Freedom Fighters *and* **Truth** Tellers

Freedom Fighters *and* Truth Tellers

Breaking Free From the Hurts Inside
So You Can Change the World Around You

Kim Gowdy

Printed in the United States of America

Published by Author Academy Elite
PO Box 43, Powell, OH 43035
www.AuthorAcademyElite.com

ISBN-13: 9781943526055
ISBN-10: 1943526052

Unless otherwise indicated, Scripture quotations are from THE HOLY BIBLE, NEW INTERNATIONAL VERSION®, NIV® Copyright © 1973, 1978, 1984, 2011 by Biblica, Inc.™ Used by permission. All rights reserved worldwide.

Scripture quotations marked (NIV) are from THE HOLY BIBLE, NEW INTERNATIONAL VERSION®, NIV® Copyright © 1973, 1978, 1984, 2011 by Biblica, Inc.™ Used by permission. All rights reserved worldwide.

Scripture quotations marked (NLT) are taken from the *Holy Bible*, New Living Translation, copyright ©1996, 2004, 2007, 2013 by Tyndale House Foundation. Used by permission of Tyndale House Publishers, Inc., Carol Stream, Illinois 60188. All rights reserved.

Scripture quotations marked (The Message) are taken from THE MESSAGE. Copyright © by Eugene H. Peterson 1993, 1994, 1995, 1996, 2000, 2001, 2002. Used by permission of NavPress. All rights reserved. Represented by Tyndale House Publishers, Inc.

The Internet addresses, email addresses, and phone numbers in this book are accurate at the time of publication. They are provided as a resource. Kim Gowdy or the publisher do not endorse them or vouch for their content or permanence.

DEDICATION

To my loving and generous husband, Doug, and our precious children, Grace and John.

CONTENTS

It takes one generation to break the cycle of hurt, turn their hearts toward God, and be free to live out their God-given destiny. These brave Freedom Fighters and Truth Tellers pass on a legacy of faith and God's love to their children and the next generation. It takes only one. Be the one to stand and fight.

FOREWORD

THE WORLD NEEDS more people like Kim Gowdy. She's a giver and a trailblazer, and—as you'll soon discover—she's also a Freedom Fighter and Truth Teller.

You probably understand the giver part. She's never short on dishing out sincere compliments and strategic prayers offered on your behalf.

The trailblazer part?

She's willing to jump in and cut a path of adventure and risk. She's also made it a daily habit to truly live. The alternative doesn't sound too appealing, and yet so many choose slow death rather than abundant life.

But now for the Freedom Fighter part.

She's a warrior, not in the "I'm going to kill you" way but more in the "I'm going to confront the lies that are killing you" way. She cares deeply about you and your freedom—so much that she'll fight with you and for you until you experience it personally.

Translation? Don't let your self-limiting beliefs get in her way. She'll call them out as she lifts you up.

And finally for the Truth Teller part.

Until you've written a book, you don't know how much sacrifice it takes. Writing is like creating new life. When Kim told me she wanted to write this book, I immediately knew the source of her motivation. She believes that Truth sets people free. More than influence, impact, or income, Kim wants to see souls set free—specifically yours.

Freedom Fighters and Truth Tellers is just that. You're about to embark on a transformational journey of hope. This book is her gift to you. She's trail blazed a path, and she won't rest until you've discovered the truth—that you were created to experience true freedom.

Kary Oberbrunner
CEO of Redeem the Day and Igniting Souls
Co-creator of Author Academy Elite
Author of *Day Job to Dream Job, The Deeper Path*, and *Your Secret Name*

INTRODUCTION

Wow, I'm SO glad you are here! Please don't think it's weird that I've been thinking about you since I discovered this unexpected dream to write a book. If it could get any more awkward, I have to tell you that you are also part of what I call my BIG DREAM—well, you and some other people I care about.

If you read the Foreword of my book, you met my coach and mentor, Kary Oberbrunner. I attended one of his author workshops two and a half years ago and had no idea I would end up on this adventurous path. Up until then, I thought my journal writing was between God and me. What I did not know is that writing and sharing my freedom story with others is a significant part of WHO and WHY I was created to be.

I spoke with someone recently who told me she was not able to get into a book I had told her about. She mentioned in the introduction the person was just too happy, and it was a barrier that kept her from reading any further. This made me sad because I think the content may have helped her break some unhealthy cycles in her life. It may not have however; it's just a thought confirmed by the resistance she was receiving in not wanting to move forward.

It turns out the author of this particular book has really impacted my life. I get her happiness and her thankfulness. She would be the first to tell you she has been set free from a bunch of lies and self-limiting beliefs. I, too, was an unidentified captive who, through grace and mercy, was lovingly set free.

You may connect with the way I write and share my story, or you may not. I think it's a good thing if you know my message does not resonate with you, because this may be the reason why the world needs to hear your story. There are people who will connect with how you share your journey, and there will be people who do not. The people that do need YOU!

Like me, you may be someone who has or is finding your voice and ways to share your unique message with the world. I'm excited for what is in store in the pages to come. My hope is that through reading my story and my invitation to share yours, you will be inspired and encouraged to take some next steps.

Before we get started, I have to be honest and up front with you. I'm not qualified to write this book. What I mean is that I am not a trained writer or particularly skilled at grammar, although I know an editor who is amazing at it. I'm not a licensed counselor, although I've personally benefited from counseling. I'm not qualified in that I don't have a Bible college degree, although I have been mentored and taught by many who do. I'm no real expert on prayer or spiritual disciplines, although I have journeyed with and served others, and I have seen God perform miracles in and through people like me.

What I am an expert on is my own story. And so are you. You are the expert on your story. We are meant to hear and share our hero stories so others can find themselves in them. There are people who are waiting to hear how your story can inspire and help them. And there are people who need to be a part of your own big dream.

Having worked in a high-performing, competitive investment environment, I've learned about climbing the corporate ladder. In my life, I've climbed two ladders and journeyed on two paths. The first path focused on freedom on the outside. The second has made all the difference—pursuing freedom on the inside.

This is not a self-help book. I've read many in the past. This is a God-helps book. The difference in perspective may appear subtle to some, but it has resulted in a dramatic change in my life as well as in the lives of those I love and care about around me. Some of my decisions in the past were made out of a place of fear, which, for the most part, did not serve me well. I noticed radical life transformation when I began to see my choices through the lens of faith—not faith in something or even myself but faith in someone greater, who came to rescue and set captives like me FREE and set on a new path of victory.

I often think of my journey as *before* Jesus and *after* Jesus. The *before*—identified by perceived status and riches. The *after*—a different kind of identity and wealth. If you ask me any day of the week which I would choose, my hope is you will find the answer in the pages of this book.

At the end of each chapter, I've created an intentional space for you called "Your Sacred Time, Space, and Calling." Here you will find freedom exercises, questions, study tools, prayers, and encouragement that I've found helpful over the years. My hope is that the exercises are life-giving to you and are helpful on your journey. Personally, my best and most intimate conversations with God are when I journal and write. The more you talk with God and actually listen for what He is saying to you, the more you will be in tune with His voice. You may want to use your own notebook or journal, or I've allowed space for you to write directly in this book.

You will also have an opportunity to discover what God is saying to you through an easy and practical Bible study method that I and others have found to be life-changing. You will need a Bible—either a physical Bible (I personally like to use New International Version [NIV] or New Living Translation [NLT]) or one you can access online through sites like YouVersion (www.youversion.com) and Bible Gateway (www.biblegateway.com).

If you are not sure or you don't believe there is a God, that's okay. It's okay to not be okay. I hope you are inspired to read my story and, in turn, to share your own story with others. If this is the case for you, can I ask you something? Would you consider asking God to show up in your life? Would you think about saying out loud right now something like, "God, if you are real, will you reveal yourself to me in a tangible and flashing lights kind of way?"

What if the Creator of Heaven and Earth showed up in your life?

What if you discovered you are not alone in your pain, hurt, and struggles?

What if you connected to a Great Love, who adores you and is calling your name?

What if you could really be yourself with God?

What if you discovered, as a result, WHO and WHY you were created to be on this earth?

What do you have to lose by asking?

What do you have to gain?

What a gift to have this opportunity to journey with you. I'm excited for you. I'm praying for you. I have friends who are praying for you as I write this book. You are loved and cared for by a God who I hope you know has an amazing plan for your life. I pray He will bring genuine people to come alongside you and to encourage and mentor you. Look for them. They may already be people you know who are waiting for you to ask them to share their story with you.

Kim Gowdy

PART I—CAGED

"Fear can hold you prisoner. Hope can set you free."

SHAWSHANK REDEMPTION

CAGED IS WHERE you feel trapped, burdened, and overwhelmed. There is pain, hurt, and conflict in your life that you are convinced will never go away. You may lack freedom in your relationships and circumstances that you wish you had. You may be paralyzed by fear in your life and the lies you believe about yourself.

So many of us live here. Whether we are aware of it or not, these stuck places keep us locked up inside and prevent us from moving forward and living the lives intended for us.

Does it have to be this way? It's been said that the definition of insanity is doing the same thing over and over and expecting a different result.

Is there hope? Can things really change?

1

PAIN IN THE PILES

"Anything of value has this rhythm to it: pain first, payoff later. If we face the pain early, the payoff will come. And the converse is true as well: If we avoid the pain now, the payoff will never come. And more pain will."

DR. HENRY CLOUD

"KIM, THIS IS really bad. There's been a break-in. I haven't seen anything like this before…the way they broke in to your apartment…and the mess they made…um…it's not good."

I arrived at the building and saw my landlord waiting for me at the front door. "Your neighbors heard everything and were too scared to do anything," she informed me.

Seeing the shock on my face, the policeman at the top of the elevator told me the burglars had used an effective tool—something a body shop uses to take dents out of car doors. They punched through my door and made a very large hole, leaving woodchips scattered throughout the hallway.

"Could they have been looking for something of great value?" the policeman asked.

I stood stunned, still numb from the uninvited ordeal.

He continued. "Look, this doesn't appear to be a random break-in."

I finally found my words. "I'm not sure what they were looking for."

By this point, I felt incredibly uncomfortable for a number of reasons. Maybe I should have been concerned about what was stolen, but something else was on my mind. My apartment was a real MESS. The robbers had gone through everything. But I have to admit, my apartment was a mess not just because of the robbers.

The truth is, much of the mess was created by me.

Imagine piles of laundry on the floor.

Imagine piles of dishes in the kitchen.

Imagine piles of junk on the living room floor.

I lived on my own, and I often had a cleaning lady come to just keep me accountable so I wouldn't let my apartment get this messy. Sadly, this was not one of those times.

Something inside me allowed this mess into my life. I didn't question it. I just lived in the mess. I didn't say anything to anyone about the state of my apartment that day. I just stood there—trapped, exposed, and speechless.

I felt like there was this oversized elephant in the room.

I felt sick to my stomach.

I felt frozen inside.

Speaking of elephants, have you heard of elephant thinking?[1] It's taken from the concept of how baby elephants are trained by the circus. It's called straining, where the animal is chained to a pole in the ground. Of course the baby elephant wants to get away; however, when they pull on the chain, they aren't able to escape. Eventually, the baby elephant gives up and stops trying.

As the animal grows, he could easily get away, but he makes no effort. He assumes he's trapped. This was me on that particular day. I saw no way to escape because I didn't know I needed to break free from anything. The messes in my life were symptoms of the pain and the hurt on the inside of me.

That night and the months to follow, I feared living on my own in my apartment. I feared the robbers would come back. I felt horrible and violated that someone had gone through every inch of my home despite all my messes. It took a few days for my door to be replaced. There was a patched hole in my apartment door and an even bigger hole in my scared and broken heart.

"You might want to consider dusting because we just weren't able to take any fingerprints." Although he probably didn't mean any harm, the policeman's comment still stung. For a long time after the break-in, I kept going back to his comment. I knew I needed to do more than dusting!

Messes and piles have been a struggle my entire life. On the outside, I had a successful career, a six-figure income, and a great social life. However, on the inside, I was a mess with a mountain of unresolved hurts and wounds. I could see now how my apartment was a picture of what I looked like on the inside.

The picture that comes to mind is of a bird in a cage.

Locked up.

Trapped in.

Held down.

Not free.

Have you ever felt this way? I did—back then and even more recently in a prison cell at Shawshank Prison. More on that later, but for now, consider this quote from the film *Shawshank Redemption*:

"Some birds are not meant to be caged, that's all. Their feathers are too bright, their songs too sweet and wild. So you let them go, or when you open the cage to feed them they somehow fly out past you. And the part of you that knows it was wrong to imprison them in the first place rejoices, but still, the place where you live is that much more drab and empty for their departure."[2]

In more recent years, I've referred to the messes in my life and how I have hidden my pain in the piles. Imagine ALL my pain just sitting there at the bottom of the mayhem. It's like somehow I avoided my pain by hiding it underneath each pile and each mess.

Even years later, I've still struggled with not cleaning up the clutter around me. At times I've been stuck and unable to go through my piles to deal with the messes. I feel a particular pain. When I look at the mess, I'm reminded in a nagging way that I still have not cleaned it up. As I walk by each time, I hurt even more inside, and I'm continually reminded of the pain.

By avoiding the mess, I pretend I don't have to deal with the pain, which, in turn, just prolongs the pain. It's what my coach calls living in chronic pain versus facing the mess and the hurt buried underneath.

Throughout this book, I will talk about how I benefited from taking the journey of acute pain that only lasts for a season and brings healing and redemption with it.

I know now I had been stuck in my story. Part of the paralysis had been as a result of the deep hurt and wounds that I had no idea needed healing. It took me a while to find this out. There are choices I would have made differently back then if I had known what I know now. I can see how I had no voice for my pain and little self-awareness that my life could and needed to change.

I wish I could say that many years later, now married with children and a home, I no longer have struggles and messes in my life. However, pain is part of life, and no one is immune to it. I know now not to hide it or mask it but to see the opportunities in it. I've learned that often traveling close alongside my pain is my potential—and how I can purposely change my world around me in how I respond to the hurts and pain. It turned out to be a big shift and change in mindset for me from victim to victor.

I'm thankful for this newfound freedom and for the new tools in my toolbox to help me process life and change how I approach the messes and hurts now when they occur.

Is this something you can relate to?

Is it just me? Have you ever felt stuck in your story?

Is there a place in your life where you hide your pain?

I'm thankful for the opportunity to journey with you. Finding out more about who you were created to be is worth it. Pursuing freedom from what keeps us stuck inside is worth it. You are worth it.

One of my two favorite books in the Bible is Isaiah. God has pointed me to it and healed me through it so many times. It's the place where the Bible talks most about captivity. I was the worst kind of captive because I didn't even know I was a prisoner. I didn't know I had any other options.

Now I realize God has a bigger plan to see the people He loves set free. Here's what He tells us:

> "But now, O Jacob, listen to the LORD who created you. O Israel, the one who formed you says, 'Do not be afraid, for I have ransomed you. I have called you by name; you are mine. When you go through deep waters, I will be with you. When you go through rivers of difficulty, you will not drown. When you walk through the fire of oppression, you will not be burned up; the flames will not consume you. For I am the LORD, your God, the Holy One of Israel, your Savior. I gave Egypt as a ransom for your freedom; I gave Ethiopia and Seba in your place. Others were given in exchange for you. I traded their lives for yours because you are precious to me. You are honored, and I love you.'" (Isaiah 43:1–4 NLT)

You might wonder what the robbers took from my apartment that day. I know I was certainly curious.

Some spare change.

A pair of sunglasses.

My stereo.

A camera.

None of these things had great value.

I once heard that "God is in the business of recovering stolen property." Jesus expounded upon this thought by saying, "The enemy comes to steal, kill, and destroy, but God comes to give us life and life abundantly."[3]

As I share this story with you, the phrase GREAT VALUE really sticks out. One of my earliest memories as a child is the sense that God was telling me that I was destined for GREATNESS. I can see clearly now how God had a plan for my life and how the enemy had a plan for my life as well. Contrary to God's plan, the enemy's plan is to shame, paralyze, and destroy.

I'm thankful that God's plan for His people is for greatness. His greatness. It's up to us which one we choose. In my case, I was in a place where the enemy was having a party in my apartment and my life.

Unlike the storyline from the children's book *The Cat in the Hat* by Dr. Seuss, there was no cleaning crew to come and clean up the trail of messes in my life.

Is there something that the enemy has stolen from you in your life? Were you aware that this was even happening? It was a wake-up call for me.

So God hates robbery? Yes, here's what He says:

"Instead of your shame you will receive a double portion, and instead of disgrace you will rejoice in your inheritance. And so you will inherit a double portion in your land, and everlasting joy will be yours. 'For I, the LORD, love justice; **I hate robbery** and wrongdoing. In my faithfulness I will reward my people and make an everlasting covenant with them. Their descendants will be known among the nations and their offspring among the peoples. All who see them will acknowledge that they are a people the LORD has blessed." (Isaiah 61:7–9 NIV)

God wants to restore to you everything that the enemy has stolen in your life because He wants to speak encouragement, identity, and blessing over you. He doesn't want to shame you. He doesn't want to shame me for the messes I made in my apartment or the choices I made in my life. He wants a path to be made clear for you to inherit the double portion He has for you and for you to receive His everlasting joy.

The opposite of "steal" is to "give back." God cannot steal from us. It is not His character. One of the Ten Commandments is "Do not steal."[4] This is a topic that He takes very seriously. Theft invokes feelings of fear and insecurity. God, whose character is Love, tells us "Do not fear."[5] His generous promises to us provide an umbrella of safety and security in all circumstances.

When I think back to my apartment story, I had been in a place where I kept God at arm's length. My goals were to move forward with my life and my future, although it seemed like my past did not want to let me go. I felt like an imposter in that on the outside it appeared as though I had everything together. The truth being that as the messes manifested in ways like in my apartment, it was really a reflection of what was going on in the inside.

I made excuses and attributed my messiness as a response to growing up in a home that was excessively clean. I wasn't aware or willing to look beneath the surface to see what was really going on. I didn't know I had emotional and spiritual needs that weren't being met. I didn't have the emotional intelligence or spiritual wisdom to get myself unlocked from my reality.

What I needed was God to help me. When I came to this realization and went through the life-changing process that He had for me, my healing accelerated. Awareness came—awareness replaced with hope then healing and freedom and an amazing gift of purpose on the other side.

This book is about how God transformed my life from the inside out.

Cleaning up one mess at a time.

Healing one hurt at a time.

Taking one baby step at a time.

As my journey unfolds, God is turning my messes into a masterpiece. He's using my hurts and redeeming them. He's generously giving me a message to share.

I'm glad you're here. My hope is that you're encouraged and inspired to find your voice, look at the hurts and messes in your life, and share your story and message with the world.

What God did for me, He will do for you. His promises are lasting and good. They do not expire.

The journey to wholeness and freedom isn't an easy one. There will be messes along the way that need to be revealed for what they are and cleaned up. Deal with one mess at a time. Ask God to help you with each mess and each hurt. He is waiting for you to ask. Freedom is on the other side of every mess, and therefore it's worth pursuing. It's worth pushing through. It's worth fighting for what matters. I'm praying for you and your journey.

Remember, God is in the business of recovering stolen property. He wants to come close to you. He's reaching out for your hand. He is there to help you each step of the way. He wants to restore what has been stolen from you and give you more than you can ever imagine.

In writing this book, I wanted to create an intentional space for you to connect with God. I'm calling it "Your Sacred Time, Space, and Calling" because it is just for you. It is intended to be a place to think, pray, and reflect in a meaningful way.

At the end of each chapter, you will find freedom exercises, devotional tools, and prayer strategies that have helped me. I hope these exercises are encouraging and beneficial to you on your journey.

Sure, I can share my journey and how God has redeemed and transformed my life, but I also want you to see this happen in your life. Perhaps you have already experienced healing and freedom, and you are wondering:

"Is this it for me?"

"Is there more?"

I believe, on this side of heaven, there's always more freedom available to us. More freedom for you and more freedom for me. You may be thinking what I'm saying about God redeeming my life is okay for me but not for you—or maybe it even sounds a bit crazy. You may be wondering, where is God? Is there a God? And if there is a Creator, what can He do for me?

All I know is that I needed to come to the end of myself before I even understood freedom was a possibility.

My genuine desire is simple—by sharing my story, I want to encourage you. I want to help you save some time and avoid some of the mistakes I made.

God hears you. He understands what you're going through, and He deeply cares for you.

YOUR SACRED TIME, SPACE, AND CALLING

15-MINUTE FREEDOM EXERCISE

On a piece of paper or in your journal, draw a picture of yourself. It's okay if you don't consider yourself to be an artist. You can draw a stick person. This is what I did.

Then, as you look at the picture, ask yourself the question—where am I experiencing or hiding my pain? If you are not sure, that is okay. Remember my story? I hid my pain in the piles—at the bottom of the mess—and I know from experience that when you hide something, you can't always find it.

If you are not sure about the question, ask God if and where you are hiding your pain. You can simply say, "Lord, where am I hiding my pain?" Place a mark or an X where you are experiencing the most pain. There is no right or wrong answer. This is just for you.

When I first did this exercise, I discovered that I had been hiding my pain in my core—both literally and figuratively. I will talk more about your core later in another chapter.

Healing comes when we find a voice for our pain. This is a process. This exercise is meant to help you take your pain out of hiding so to speak. So what is next? First, don't do this alone. Have a conversation with a trusted friend or perhaps even a good counselor. I've personally benefitted from my time with a counselor. The world says we're weak if we ask for help. I think the opposite. I think we display strength, character, and maturity when we ask for help.

When you can identify where your pain is, you can begin to take steps toward the healing process found in God Himself. You can also take steps toward embracing your purpose and potential.

SPECIAL TIME WITH GOD

Set aside 15 minutes. At the end of each chapter, I've picked a psalm for you to consider reading and reflecting on. I'll share with you more about the Book of Psalms—my other favorite book in the Bible—as we go along. Read **PSALM 40** in the Old Testament. You may prefer reading it a second time out loud. What verse sticks out or connects with you? Apply the SOAP Method (Please see Appendix A for more information on this easy 4-Step Bible Journal Method).

S – Scripture – Write out the verse you chose. Write it in this space below or in your journal.

_____

_____

_____

O – Observation – What are one or two facts that you observe from the verse you chose?

_____

_____

_____

A – Application – How can you personally apply this verse to your life?

_____

_____

_____

P – Prayer – Write out a prayer to God related to your reading today. There is no right or wrong way to do this. Prayer is having a conversation with God. Think of this as a conversation starter between you and God.

_____

_____

_____

PRAYER AND ENCOURAGEMENT

It's been said that the areas of our deepest pain can be the areas where we have the **greatest impact** in the world.

What is one **mess or hurt** in your life that comes to mind?

_____

_____

_____

Does the idea of hiding your pain in the piles resonate with you? Or **how would you describe** your pain story? If you are not sure, it's okay; we will be talking more about this as we journey along.

_____

_____

_____

Pray! There is no right or wrong way to pray. Prayer is simply having a conversation with God, who loves you and wants to spend time with you. My prayer life changed dramatically when I shared my pain and hurts with God and really engaged in an honest conversation with Him. What can you bring to prayer and conversation with God and ask for His wisdom, guidance, and help with today? Are you in a place where you can say, "God, I give you my pain, hurts, messes...please help me, please heal and encourage me, and bring others alongside me to help care for my heart. Help me take a closer look at where I hide my pain and possibly my potential to impact the world around me."

2

CRY FOR HELP

"To what will you look for help if you will not look to that
which is stronger than yourself?"

C.S. LEWIS

I CRIED OUT, LOOKING up in the night's sky, "GOD, I'm done! I'm finished!"
"No more. I can't. I know you have a plan and a purpose for my life, but I'm
telling you, God, you need to work this out. You know my heart. You know if
there is someone out there for me. He may be just around the corner. I don't
know. You know, God. You have to do this because I can't anymore."

The pain felt unbearable. Another failed relationship. Dumped on my couch—
again! This, a third long-term relationship in a decade, failed. This time there were
plans for marriage. He had asked my parents for my hand and their blessing.

HURT on top of HURT piled on top of HURT. Unhealthy relationships
in every area of my life. My issues were a cocktail of constant inner struggle
to control others while feeling a lack of control and an unknown pit of people
pleasing to gain approval from others.

Exhausting—I'm so done!

This was the day, out of complete desperation, that I came to the end of myself.

If you've heard of David in the Bible, you know he is someone who cried out to God for help on many occasions. Here he wrote in the Book of Psalms—

"In my distress I called to the LORD; I cried to my God for help. From his temple he heard my voice; my cry came before him, into his ears." (Psalm 18:6 NIV)

"The righteous cry out, and the LORD hears them; he delivers them from all their troubles." (Psalm 34:17 NIV)

If David were here chatting with us, I think he would be the first to say he didn't always get it right, and in fact, he often found himself in a boatload of trouble by his own doing and direct disobedience to God. And yet, when he cried out, God heard and helped him out.

David, someone known as a man after God's own heart, wrote most of the psalms and, I think, modeled well the importance of having ongoing conversations with God about the highs and lows we experience in life. He asked for God's help on a regular basis and shared a whole range of emotions—both positive and negative. His honesty with God is refreshing, and I think it gives us permission to do the same.

Have you ever cried out to God in the night's sky? Did you know you could even do this? Maybe you are in a place where, like I was, you are "done" with a situation you are in. Can I leave you with this encouragement? Know you are not alone. Know that you can cry out to God at any time. He knows your heart. He hears you. He's waiting to help you.

My hope is you are encouraged to start your own conversations with God. If this is something you are already doing, this is wonderful—keep going. This morning I found myself challenged with this question: "Would you be willing to take your conversation with God to a deeper level?" The question came from a dear friend who helped me work through some negative feelings I had been experiencing this week. I thought I had it all figured out. And then we invited Him into our conversation, and it made all the difference as He helped me identify what was going on underneath the surface.

Lasting transformation happens when we cry out to God and ask for help. I spent a decade of my life trying to fix my problems and perform away my difficulties. For me personally, self-help books and their practices did not work in the long run. In fact, in some cases, they even made my problems worse. When I shifted my perspective to God-helps and His direction for my life, it made all the difference as I found genuine solutions to my struggles.

Asking God for help is the first step and the next step and the next—and, really, the necessary step in growing in your faith and having a deeper, intimate relationship with Him.

Have you ever learned a skill to the point where you've mastered it and you no longer needed to study it? This is where I think David the psalmist challenges us in his honest conversations with his Creator—that we will never be in a place where we will master life and not need to ask for God's help.

You may be asking—really? Is God really there? Or you may be wondering, is it okay to say exactly what I'm thinking and feeling with Him?

A friend questioned, "Can I really do this?" She went on to say, "I thought God was only interested in hearing about my positive feelings."

Another friend shared, "I've never talked with God about my pain. I only go to Him to ask for help for someone else. Not for me. I don't ever pray for myself. I pray for other people."

Let me explain further. There are psalms written by David called the Imprecatory Psalms. Examples are Psalm 69 and Psalm 109. These are not often talked about in church on a Sunday morning. The "imprecatory psalms" are prayer songs of a particularly vigorous attitude toward the enemy. The verb "imprecate" means "to pray evil against."[1]

If you read Psalm 69, David goes on as much to ask God to not be merciful and to take out his enemies.

"Save me, O God, for the floodwaters are up to my neck. Deeper and deeper I sink into the mire; I can't find a foothold. I am in deep water, and the floods overwhelm me. I am exhausted from crying for help; my throat is parched. My eyes are swollen with weeping, waiting for my God to help me. Those who hate me without cause outnumber the hairs on my head. Many enemies try to destroy me with lies, demanding that I give back what I didn't steal…. Pile their sins up high, and don't let them go free. Erase their names from the Book of Life; don't let them be counted among the righteous." (Psalm 69:1–4, 27–28 NLT)

Wow. Can you imagine saying something like "erase their names from the Book of Life" to God? If you can, that's awesome. Continue having those "keeping it real" conversations.

If it's a stretch for you, that's okay. Crying out to God in this way may not come as naturally to you as it did for King David. I know for myself that I did not identify with how I was feeling and tended to stuff my pain and negative emotions down. I held God at arm's length and did life my way until I arrived at the point where I couldn't do it anymore.

Personally speaking, the deep pain in my life, whether I could voice it or was even willing to admit it, came through my relationships. I thought this was the way it is in relationships, and I looked to my coping mechanisms for the answers and to numb my pain. Remember I just mentioned my own pit of people pleasing?

Does any of what I've shared resonate with you? What is coming to mind when you read this chapter? Do you feel overwhelmed or the need to cry out to God about a relationship or circumstance in your life?

Sometimes we can get stuck in our own story. I know I did. We may be thinking about our hurt and pain and where we feel caged or trapped. It is like we are experiencing pain, and yet we do not have a voice and a way to express it.

You may be asking, "Why would I express my feelings to God?" Or you may see God as distant and up there somewhere and your life is down here and you like it that way—so no need to get Him involved, right? Or maybe you didn't know you could have a conversation with God about your feelings. As a result, we may look for ways to:

Mask our pain.

Hide from our pain.

Avoid our pain.

Stuff our pain.

Not acknowledge there is pain.

Ignore our pain.

Numb our pain.

Rationalize our pain away.

Fill in the blank here.

If we don't deal with the hurt or express our pain, this can turn into an addictive cycle—the pain continues, and we experience chronic pain. Chronic pain is described in Webster's dictionary as pain being marked by a long duration or frequent recurrence.

What if we choose to face the pain, give our pain a voice, ask for help, pursue freedom from our pain, be open, and look at the areas of our hearts that need healing? Here, we find this path can be painful as well. This process can be described as experiencing acute pain and yet purposeful and short term in nature.

The truth is, we can't avoid pain. I heard Chet Scott, someone who coaches CEOs and builds leaders, share, "We can choose chronic pain and live with it for a lifetime or we can choose acute pain, which only lasts for a while, and we receive a lifetime of benefit."[2]

How do you find a voice for your pain?

Think about how David expressed his emotions. He wrote psalms to God. Consider writing out your own psalm or letter to God. Maybe you are saying, "But I can't do that." Stick with me here as we keep going.

If you are like me, you may have a desire to know Jesus and have a deeper relationship with Him. From what I've experienced, this happens when we are honest and are willing to look beneath the surface to see what is really going on.

I went through a period of time last year when I really didn't like when people said, "Hi, how are you?" The truth is I was struggling and having a really hard time. In that season, I'd respond by saying, "I'm not doing so well," or "I'm okay. How are you?" I think some people didn't know how to respond, maybe because we are so used to saying and hearing, "I'm great! How are you?"

After decades of people pleasing and saying what I thought people would want to hear, I now much prefer to keep it real and honest. And I think God does as well. He knows what you are going through, and He's waiting to respond in truth and love to you.

Start by telling God how you are feeling. Think about having an unpretending conversation with Him. If you are not sure how you are feeling, say, "I am not feeling anything," or "I'm not sure." Shout at Him if you need to. Cry out in the night sky like I did. Say whatever you need to say in whatever way you need to say it.

You can do this in the form of a prayer, which is really a two-way conversation with God. Here we have the opportunity to speak with Him and, more importantly, listen for the truth and encouragement He wants to speak over us.

The other option, which is one of my favorites, is to journal your conversation. Start by setting aside fifteen minutes. Take out a journal or a piece of paper. Write at the top your page "My Psalm to God." Share how you are feeling—both positive and negative feelings. Ask Him for help where you are in need. Share your pain. What are the feelings, if any, that are coming to the surface even as you are reading this sentence? Share these feelings as you journal. Ask God to speak to you through your hurt and pain. Ask Him to speak to you through how you are feeling. God lovingly encourages and convicts us.

Any accusing thoughts are not from Him, and you can ask God to help you hear His voice and His alone.

I have to say, there is something that happens when we put pen to paper. Often I find journaling helps bring clarity and process to the stuck areas in my life. For me personally, I feel a closer connection with God when I write and journal. It's something that really encourages me and fills me up.

I have a question for you. What do you think—is it okay to express a negative emotion, like anger, to God? In the Bible, in the Book of Ephesians, it says:

> "'In your anger do not sin': Do not let the sun go down while you are still angry, and do not give the devil a foothold." (Ephesians 4:26–27 NIV)

The writer, the Apostle Paul, is saying that when you are angry, do not sin. He's not saying it is a sin to be angry or to express your anger in a way that is helpful in understanding it.

Remember King David, a man after God's own heart, and how he freely expressed his feelings? Think about if we are angry and we don't talk about it—what happens? Again, we see the patterns and tendencies that are not healthy for us take root. A good question to ask is, what is behind the anger? Some questions I've asked myself are—

Is my anger directed towards my circumstances?

Is my anger directed towards my relationships?

Or just maybe am I deep down angry at God?

Say what you need to say to God. He can take it. If you are angry, tell Him. If you feel you have been forgotten or betrayed by God, tell Him. He's waiting to have an honest conversation with you. We are not meant to journey the highs and lows of life alone and without God. This is when real transformation happens. You can do it today. You are not alone. Don't do this alone. Reach out and ask someone to pray for you or with you—think of a trusted friend or someone you know who prays. I'm praying for you too.

When I cried out in the night's sky, I felt like God was waiting for me. I had a deep sense He heard me. I experienced a release of some sort. A weight lifted off my shoulders, and something changed inside me. I noticed it right away. My heart turned towards God in a new and intentional way. Through my honesty and desperation, God sacredly exchanged my confusion, discouragement, and fear for His clarity, hope, and peace that dark night and many times since then.

He's waiting for you too. He hears you. He cares for and understands you. His response to you is truthful, loving, gracious, and kind. What clarity, hope, and peace does your Creator have for you? Be courageous and ask Him.

"Hear me as I pray, O LORD. Be merciful and answer me! My heart has heard you say, 'Come and talk with me.' And my heart responds, 'LORD, I am coming.'" (Psalm 27:7–8 NLT)

This experience of coming to the end of myself and desperately crying out to God filled me with a new sense of hope and direction for my life. It began my journey back to God and, thankfully, the life He intended for me.

My story since then has been a process with many highs and lows. I won't sugarcoat anything—it's been a long journey and not always easy. I'm thankful that through it, God has used it to grow and shape my character. My hope in sharing my story is that others are encouraged, and if in any way I can help you on your journey, maybe you can avoid mistakes I've made or delays I've experienced.

Recently a friend asked me, "Why do you think this is the case for you? Why has it been a long process for you?"

As I reflected on her questions, I thought about how God can free people in an instant. He's even given me a front row seat to witness and see such miracles and His character in them. And despite some pity parties I've thrown for myself, I'm totally okay with it now. This is my story. I can see how sharing my highs and lows is helping people who process life the way I do. Leadership expert John C. Maxwell says that an event motivates and a process matures.[3] In my case, had my freedom been just an event, I would not have had the opportunity to mature into the person God created me to be.

It's been said that the area of our deepest pain and struggle has the potential to be our greatest message and impact in the world. I can't believe I'm saying this, but I'm glad God did not waste my pain and has turned my hurts into this message. And as it turned out, my sweet husband literally lived just around the corner—but that's another story for another time.

You don't need to come to the end of yourself to connect with your Creator on a deeper level. I actually recommend you avoid it if at all possible. You can cry out to God anytime, even right now. He is waiting to meet with you and to help you in your distress. God's help is the best help.

YOUR SACRED TIME, SPACE, AND CALLING

15-MINUTE FREEDOM EXERCISE

My husband and I have this code word. Let me say he is one of the most generous and intellectual people I know. He knows a lot about topics that I know nothing about, which is great, because he often shares helpful information in conversation. There are times when I need to get his attention or he needs to get mine, and we say the word "filter," which means we think the other person is sharing too much on a particular topic with our kids, typically around the dinner table. It's kind of like a pause button, and we then talk about it with just the two of us later if we need to.

So what is the relevance of me sharing our code word with you? Imagine you can say anything to God with NO FILTER. No one is saying that's too much or you can't say that or that's inappropriate.

Yes, you can say, "God, where are you? Why is this happening to me? Where are you in this painful relationship or circumstance in my life? God, you need to work this out because I can't." Or "God, _____ (you fill in the blank here)."

I shared earlier the idea of writing your own psalm to God. Or think of it as writing a letter or having an honest conversation with Him. Take some time to write down your questions, thoughts, feelings, disappointments, sadness, failures, and successes. This is something I have found to be incredibly healing and helpful on my journey as I continue to find a voice for my pain and my story. I've set aside a place for you in Appendix B where you can write your psalm to God, or feel free to write in a notebook or journal.

SPECIAL TIME WITH GOD

Set aside 15 minutes. This has been my go-to psalm this past year. Each time I read it, it encourages me more and more. I hope this is the case for you as well. Read **PSALM 27** in the Old Testament. You may consider reading it a second time out loud. What verse sticks out or connects with you? Apply the SOAP Method.

S – Scripture – Write out the verse you chose. Write it in this space below or in your journal.

_____

_____

O – Observation – What are one or two facts that you observe from the verse you chose?

_____

_____

A – Application – How can you personally apply this verse to your life?

_____

_____

P – Prayer – Write out a prayer to God related to your reading today. There is no right or wrong way to do this. Prayer is having a conversation with God. Think of this as a conversation starter between you and God.

_____

_____

_____

PRAYER AND ENCOURAGEMENT
Life is full of **Highs** and **Lows**.

What is one area of your life where you are **doing well**?

_____

_____

_____

What is one area of your life where you are **struggling**?

_____

_____

_____

Pray! Praying does not need to be complicated. There is no right or wrong way to pray. Think of it as being as simple as having a conversation with God.

With the questions you just answered, you can start your prayer by thanking God for what is going well in your life. Then ask Him for help with your lows and where you are struggling.

If you are feeling overwhelmed in your circumstances, reach out to someone—a trusted friend or someone in your church, or if you are not part of a church, think about someone you know that is a person of faith you could talk to. Ask God to bring safe people into your life. Share your highs and lows with your family or loved ones on a regular basis. Create a space, like writing in a journal, where you can voice your joys and your pain. Reflect on the peaks and valleys in your life. We are not meant to journey the highs and lows of life alone. Celebrate your highs. Share your lows and burdens with God and others that care for you. You are significant—you are accepted and loved. Know God hears you, cares for you, and understands you.

Think about sharing your highs and lows in conversation with your friends or loved ones at dinner or with your kids at bedtime on a regular basis. Include yourself, and have each person share their high and low of the day and pray together. It may be awkward at first, but it is worth it to push through. Be sure to thank God for each of your highs, and ask Him for help with each of your lows. This type of sharing will help bring your relationship with God and the people you care about beyond the surface and to a deeper level.

3

NUMBERS AND VALUES

"Two roads diverged in a wood, and I—
I took the one less traveled by,
And that has made all the difference."

FROM THE POEM *THE ROAD NOT TAKEN* BY ROBERT FROST

I ASKED MY BRAND new husband to go to a corporate event just four days after our wedding. I know—not the most romantic thing to do.

This prominent event headlined Mr. Jack Welsh, former CEO of General Electric (GE), sitting down with Canada's national news anchor, Peter Mansbridge, for a one-on-one chat. Feeling both compelled and excited to go, I could not wait to hear what these two men would be talking about.

Okay. I'm rethinking my decision now—who would consider this to be a good thing to do on their honeymoon? Let's just call it an occupational hazard at the time. With studying companies for work and investment purposes, I followed this former CEO's management style and found it intriguing how he managed GE over the years.

Typically a setting for symphonies and concerts, this prestigious and packed out concert hall waited in anticipation to hear Jack's sought after wisdom and controversial perspective on how to manage teams effectively.

For me personally, an unexpected gift arrived for me that night. A present nothing at all like the wedding gifts we had just received. It came packaged in the form of corporate insight that addressed the heart of my situation and my desperate need for direction in my professional world.

Like a date with destiny interrupting my perfectly postured, well-dressed position, I experienced—an AHA moment, a life-defining moment, what I like to call "my head falling in my hands and then to my lap" moment.

Sitting with my incredibly gracious husband in the second row, I found myself peeking out of the corner of my eye and looking around to see if anyone showed signs of receiving the punch that came with the truth delivered to my inmost being. Could Jack be speaking directly to me? Or was this somehow God getting my attention in the middle of my busy world?

It seemed I had been waiting for this clarity for such a long time, and yet it caught me by complete surprise. I remember sitting in a church and having a similar experience two years prior. Desperate for answers, I found myself asking, "Why am I here, God? How do I get out of this work mess that is overwhelming my soul?"

In my heart of hearts, I knew inside, and yet the fear, paralysis, and confusion blocked my next steps.

The two experiences linked in some way, like stepping stones to something I'd longed for my whole life—to know the love and passion that seemed trapped inside of me. If you can, picture two ladders leaning against a building. I found myself climbing one ladder and stopping to reflect a good distance up, only to discover I had been climbing the wrong ladder. Yes, the WRONG ladder.

Like two roads or paths in front of me—did I know I had a choice? As the fog lifted, it became clear to me that the overwhelmed road I found myself on possessed a trail of second guessing, guilt, shame, asking why, taking no personal responsibility, and feeling sorry for myself due to the impact of other people's choices.

How can I stop climbing this corporate ladder and start all over again? Really, do I have enough energy for this? Would everything I worked for be lost? What will people think of me? Will they accept me? But really, I've performed for so long—I'm recognized, rewarded, and accepted here. And yet the tension between deciding and not deciding was tearing me apart.

So what motivated my choice to pursue this career? With the benefit of hindsight, it's easy for me to answer now. Despite my strategic plan, business sense, and resourcefulness, it would be pride and fear that led the charge. In leaving business school, I quickly needed a job, and fear motivated my decision to pursue this high-paying opportunity. I took the securities course the year before, which I knew I needed to get my foot in the door. With the opportunity to stay at a friend's house and some borrowed money, I traveled across the country to a place I had not been before with no contacts and a stack of resumes in hand.

Looking beneath the surface, what stood behind my determination and fueled my brave and noble efforts? Would I say I found myself in the right place at the right time? Does this really happen when you make an agreement with pride and fear? It's ironic as I share this with you when you look at my motives that brought me to this position and then my complaining to God about it. It makes me think, how hypocritical could I have been?

> Matthew 7:5 (NIV) brings my situation to light: "You hypocrite, first take the plank out of your own eye, and then you will see clearly to remove the speck from your brother's eye."

> Mark 8:36 (NIV) says, "For what does it profit a man to gain the whole world and forfeit his soul?"

Ouch! The truth is, if you make an agreement with the dark components of fear and pride, it impacts your connection with God. God does not want to see any gaps or anything standing between you and Him. He likes your company. He wants to have an intimate relationship with you and for you to reconnect to His love and grace intended for you.

No matter where you are on your faith journey, that's all it takes—a heart-to-heart chat. In my case, it was saying, "Hi, Lord, it's me. If it's okay with you, I will just come out and say it. I'm sorry, and I take responsibility for my choice to agree with fear and pride. Please forgive me and help me. Please give me all the faith and humility I need to overcome this struggle and walk this freedom road with you."

When you have an honest conversation with God, be sure to take time to listen for a response and the encouragement He wants to speak over you. I assure you, only good things can come from such a sacred exchange with your Creator.

So you may be wondering, what exactly did Jack say that was so impactful?

First, some background on his controversial management style, as cited in a *Wall Street Journal* article that reported Mr. Welsh "believes that managers should assess their employees every year, and divide them into three categories: the top 20 percent, the middle 70 percent, and the bottom 10 percent... Critics say this forced ranking undermines team-work. It encourages employees to engage in destructive and wasteful game-playing designed to ensure they get credit, or others don't."[1]

To summarize the ranking system Mr. Welsh used, the top 20% are your superstars that you need to support and reward extravagantly. The middle 70% are people you want to invest in and spend time coaching in hopes they will move to the top 20%. The bottom 10% are people you do not spend time with, and they are let go or fired right away.

As Jack elaborated on his experiences and beliefs, I could see and appreciate both sides of the controversy.

Toward the end of the conversation, Mr. Welsh described four different employee profiles and how his managers were to assess their team members to determine which profile best described them. From what he shared, this is what I understood:

1. Those employees (team members) that make the numbers (for example, sales goals, performance targets) and have good values—invest in these people. Encourage, reward, and treat them well. Don't take them for granted. These are your top employees that you want to continue to thrive and grow.
2. Those employees (team members) that do not make the numbers and have good values—take some time to invest in these people, and see how you can support them and help them grow into your top-ranked employees.
3. Those employees (team members) that do not make the numbers and do not have good values—these are people you do not have time to invest in; at GE, these employees would have been let go immediately.
4. And then he went on to describe the fourth group of people. Jack leaned in to the audience to share that...these are people who will KILL YOUR COMPANY! These are the employees (team members) that make the numbers but do not have good values.

Wow! Enter the biggest unplanned sigh of my life and my head falling in my hands and to my lap—and there you have it! Bam!

This "by invitation only" event had on its guest list some of the highest-ranked people in the financial industry. And in that moment, you could have heard a pin drop so much so that it felt like the silence didn't know what to do with itself.

Numbers and values. Where did I see myself on the list? Well, clearly the #1 category based on my performance reviews.

My reviews would not lie, would they?

Then I pictured two sets of values. Two destinies. Which set of values will I side with? What am I willing to compromise? What will I commit to and honor in my life? Where will I take a stand?

Like a bully situation on the school playground, it would appear that the bully has the power and makes the decisions. And yet it's been said that the choice of the bystander can make all the difference. What will the bystander do? Take a stand or turn a blind eye?

After my ordained time with Jack and the amazing support of my husband, I had a plan. Well, not really a plan—I had a next step and the courage and determination to trust God's plan.

My first day back at work, I requested a meeting with my manager. They were equally excited to meet and share what was on their mind. Impacted from the same event, they decided to make some changes and let go a team member that had been causing distrust and disunity. As they looked to me, I think my response would be different than the approval they were expecting.

It seemed like every cell in my body knew what I needed to say and do. Do you know that tension and how it feels between the time of making an important decision and telling the person that needs to know the outcome?

Okay, stay focused, I told myself. *Keep it simple.* Like when my son says to me in the most respectful way, "Mommy, can you say what you just said in less words?" This time I had confidence and conviction on my side. And well, basically, the nice girl in me needed to come out and "just say it!"

And then I told my boss of over a decade that I could now see, explain, and understand how my values were not being honored on this team. I told them in the most gracious way that I had outgrown my position such that my values and long-term investment philosophy were not something I was willing to compromise. Simply put, I was on the WRONG TEAM.

Making a decision can be painful. In fact, not making a decision is a decision in itself and can be equally as painful. Often we avoid making decisions because we don't want to experience the loss, and yet it delays the opportunities on the other side of our decisions.

I sensed God was working behind the scenes based on my boss's response. They responded with respect and humility, like they had been prepared in some way. They asked if I would stay for a few months, offered letters of recommendation, and hosted a party in my honor.

Higher management asked questions, and I answered them straight. No more standing by. No turning away. I was given a six-month leave with benefits and time to consider coming back to another team.

No turning back.

No second guessing my decision.

No guilt.

No shame.

God honored my next step and the next and filled me with a peace inside beyond understanding. I felt like such a heavy burden had been lifted from me.

In more recent years, I've been more intentional about taking time to identify my personal core values. If you are not at peace or feel unsettled about something, there's a possibility you are not honoring your values. Doing this essential discovery work helps you determine gaps or blind spots in your life.

One of my core values is my faith. What do you think was a blind spot for me? What is the opposite of faith? Fear and lack of trust! Sometimes what you find traveling close to what is important to you are the deterrents that will sabotage it.

Do you remember I had made an agreement with pride and fear in pursuing a high-paying job? Making a lot of money had not been a value of mine, although to others who influenced me about my future, it was. Combined with the fear of how I would support myself after school, I can tell you the exact moment I chose fear over faith, which led me down a decade-long, unsettled path.

When it comes to deciding on a path or destiny for our lives, I think we are, by design, each given a choice. In my case, I'm thankful for a second chance to discover and honor the path intended for me.

C.S. Lewis, in his book *Mere Christianity*, wrote, "Progress means getting nearer to the place you want to be. And if you have taken a wrong turn, then to go forward does not get you any nearer. If you are on the wrong road, progress means doing an about-turn and walking back to the right road; and in that case the man who turns back soonest is the most progressive man."[2]

The road I found myself on led me to a performance-based prison with high-paying benefits. In the world's eyes, I was successful. But I knew in my heart this was not my passion and purpose in life. I'm not saying that performing well and making money are bad things; I know lots of people who do so and honor their values at the same time.

On this new road, I've had the opportunity to exchange fear for faith, hope for healing, and the absence of passion and purpose for a second chance to discover and pursue it. As I reflect back, I can see that had I missed this turn or lane change, I would have only seen the tip of God's iceberg plan for my life.

Life is not so glamorous these days.

I traded invites to the finest restaurants in the city for lunch at the mall in the suburbs with our sweet kids.

I traded wearing power suits to sometimes wearing my PJs to the kids' bus stop (under a long coat of course!).

I traded my focus on what things look like on the outside for a focus on the condition of my heart and my soul on the inside.

I traded a burning desire to perform well and please others for a burning desire to pursue freedom and hopefully inspire and encourage others.

I traded temporary riches with no guarantees for eternal values and riches that are guaranteed.

I traded guilt, shame, and regret for authenticity, hope, and peace in my heart that is beyond what I can explain.

Matthew 6:20–21 (NIV) says, "But store up for yourselves treasures in heaven, where moths and vermin do not destroy, and where thieves do not break in and steal. For where your treasure is, there your heart will be also."

Have you ever found it challenging to make an important decision in your life? Does the choice of two roads, two paths, two ladders, or two sets of values resonate with you? Have you ever wondered when facing a fork in the road, which path you will you choose? What are you willing to compromise? What will you commit to and honor in your life? Where will you take a stand?

I leave you with some verses from the Bible that I pray almost every day. They state my intention and declare the best decision I have ever made in my life. These words remind me of the new path I chose all those years ago and the life and hope I have encountered along the way.

"Show me your ways, LORD, teach me your paths. Guide me in your truth and teach me, for you are God my Savior, and my hope is in you all day long." (Psalm 25:4–5 NIV)

I pray you are encouraged in some way and that you experience the hope, confidence, life, and peace intended for you. Oh, and that you get to see it—God's iceberg plan for YOU!

YOUR SACRED TIME, SPACE, AND CALLING

15-MINUTE FREEDOM EXERCISE

Some say the secret to success is knowing what you want. What I've found helpful in determining my own core values is taking some time to journal about this question: "What do I want?" Often we find that our values are linked to our dreams and our dreams to our life purpose. Schedule fifteen minutes this week and journal, asking yourself these questions: "What do I desire for my life? What do I value most? In what direction do I want to be going?" When you've done this, then take some time to reflect on the road you are on—what motivates your choices and actions? Ask yourself this imperative question: "Are my actions aligned with what I value most?" It's okay if they're not. Now you know. Ask God to help you narrow the gaps and lead you on the right road to His plans and purposes for your life.

SPECIAL TIME WITH GOD
Set aside 15 minutes. Read **PSALM 25** in the Old Testament. This is a psalm that God has used to minister to me over the years. I pray it is a source of encouragement to you. You may consider reading it a second time out loud. What verse in Psalm 25 sticks out or connects with you? Apply the SOAP Method.

S – Scripture – Write out the verse you chose. Write it in this space below or in your journal.

_____
_____
_____

O – Observation – What are one or two facts that you observe from the verse you chose?

_____
_____

A – Application – How can you personally apply this verse to your life?

_____
_____

P – Prayer – Write out a prayer to God related to your reading today. There is no right or wrong way to do this. Prayer is having a conversation with God. Think of this as a conversation starter between you and God.

_____
_____
_____

PRAYER AND ENCOURAGEMENT
Some choices lead to **life**, and some lead to **regret**.

We all have parts of our lives we would like to go back and do over. Guilt and shame are like gifts that keep on giving. Know they are not from God.

God can and wants to redeem these areas for you. No problem or situation is too difficult for God. I don't know about you, but I am certain that Jesus came to this earth to fix my poor choices and sin problem. He can fix yours too! It starts with an honest conversation.

What is one choice you regret from the past that you would like to **share with God** and ask Him to **redeem**?

_____

_____

_____

Take some time to share with God your **feelings and struggles** and where you need some help.

_____

_____

_____

Pray! Prayer is a two-way conversation with God. In this chapter, I shared how I prayed, asking God to help me with my problem and struggle with fear and pride. Would you consider praying a similar prayer? If you are in a place of struggle or in the process of making an important decision for your life, ask God for His help, wisdom, and guidance. Remember to reach out and ask a trusted friend, pastor, or Christ follower to pray with and for you. We are thankful to be a part of a caring small group at our church and are encouraged that we are only an email or phone call away and can reach out to each other for prayer and support.

4

FACE TO FACE

"I sought the LORD, and he answered me; he delivered me from all
my fears. Those who look to him are radiant; their faces are never
covered with shame."

(PSALM 34:4–5 NIV)

IT IS NOT a journey anyone wants to take. One late Sunday night, I found
myself driving to our local hospital. As I backed out of our driveway, I
sensed fear swarming around me. I knew something was not right. I just
wanted someone to tell me everything would be okay.

As I drove through my quiet and dark neighborhood, I thought about
how my three-month ultrasound was scheduled for next week. I felt a bond
and a deep sense of love and gratitude for our baby inside of me.

This pregnancy felt similar to my first in that I felt terribly nauseous all
the time—so much so that I remembered to bring some soda crackers with
me just in case I felt sick.

Soon I found myself parked and walking into the emergency department.
The wait time to see the triage nurse, combined with the fear and nervous

feelings I felt inside, seemed like the most painful and longest wait. Then my turn came.

She wore a green uniform. I thought of a TV show I once watched where they wore similar army-green attire. Her head was down most of the time as she spoke to me. No eye contact. She asked me a number of questions. I wanted to ask her some questions, although her body language made it clear it was not part of the process.

Inside, I felt scared and tried to focus on holding back the tears.

I wondered about the reasoning behind her disengagement—had she been tired from a long shift, or did she know something I didn't? I felt this wall between her and me—maybe she did not want to go near my pain. Maybe I was a reminder of pain.

Inside, I just wanted her to look at me and say everything would be all right. *Would someone please tell me...your precious baby will be okay!*

The nurse made arrangements for some tests and instructed me to go to the waiting room. The feelings coming to the surface were overwhelming. Every worst case scenario crossed my mind. Fear fought to consume me.

I felt the absence of my husband beside me, although in some way, I felt a comfort, knowing he was caring for our sweet daughter at home, who was asleep and unaware of this ordeal. Fear continued to look for me like a lion stalks its prey.

Sitting there patiently, I waited for the nurse to call my name. And then something interrupted my thinking. Instead of fear, I chose to cling to a greater presence that night. In my heart, I prayed and asked God to wait this long wait with me—to talk me through this scary time.

Surprisingly, I did not feel alone. As I communicated with Him back and forth, minute by minute, I quietly declared, *I trust you, God, regardless of what happens.*

Was I really saying this?

What about my precious baby?

And what about my plan to have our second child by a certain age?

Okay, back to trusting God. I prayed for our baby, remembering that God loves this child even more than I do. I wondered if they knew how much I loved him or her, and would he or she know how much God loves them? My thoughts then went to our precious daughter at home and how being her mom had been the best thing I'd ever done in my life—how she made me a mom, how I was picked to be her mom, and how God made a beautiful way despite all my choices in the past.

Quite a bit of time had passed, and then I heard my name called to go for a blood test and an ultrasound. The ultrasound technician did not say much or even smile or make much eye contact with me.

Really, was this happening again?

I just wanted her to say my baby would be okay.

Could I remain hopeful?

Was I in denial?

Would I "really" trust God whatever the outcome?

After the tests, I settled back in to the waiting room. Then, after another long period of time, a nurse came to ask me to move to a patient room. More waiting. Fear, like an uninvited guest, followed me to each room.

Fear of not seeing my baby.

Fear of my baby not being okay.

Fear of my baby not knowing they're wanted.

Fear of my baby not knowing they're loved.

Fear of my baby not knowing that God loves them.

Fear of not having another baby.

Still clinging to God. Hanging on to hope. Holding back the tears.

Now sitting on a hospital bed, waiting, I saw the triage nurse walking towards me. The army-green uniform helped me make the connection quickly. I wondered how she had time to leave her desk with the extended line of people waiting.

Was this the same person who had asked me questions a number of hours before?

She went on to say, "The doctor on duty does not have the best bedside manner, and I wanted to be the one to share the results with you."

My heart sank. She asked if she could sit beside me on the bed. She looked at me, now face-to-face. I saw tenderness in her eyes. She revealed that I had a silent miscarriage, which meant my baby's heartbeat had stopped and the baby had stopped growing. She continued to share that my next steps would be to meet with a specialist who would be coming to see me soon, and she assured me that I would be in good hands.

The held-back tears came rushing down like a never ending flood. They came and they came, almost uncontrollably, as I cried out loudly for the loss of our baby. There are even more tears as I write and share this story with you.

Lost was the hope of our baby being okay. How would our baby know that they are loved?

God, would you tell my baby for me?

How would our baby know they were wanted and cared for?

Was it a boy or a girl?

How did this happen?

Was it something I did?

So many questions. More grief and pain rising from inside of me—it felt unbearable and hard to breath. The mixture of the florescent lights above combined with my unending stream of tears—it seemed like somehow my contact lenses had been replaced with tiny razor blades burning my eyes. So much pain.

The doctor came and spoke with me. I asked if it was possible they made a mistake. He responded no and recommended I go for surgery as soon as possible. He said he would be looking for a doctor that would be available the next day. I needed to go home and come back and wait another long wait until my time could be scheduled. He assured me that I would be in the best of care.

A woman came from the other side of the curtain to speak with me. She spoke softly and asked if she could sit with me for a while. She confided how she had a miscarriage in between her daughter and son; in fact, she had just told them about it a couple of weeks prior.

"I know you don't know me, but can I hug you?" she asked.

As I received her welcomed hug, I felt something that is really hard to explain. It's just a feeling I had. Like somehow God was hugging me through this gracious woman. It didn't feel weird or anything. I felt through her, in some way, His loving embrace, hope, and peace in the midst of this heart-breaking news.

Psalm 34:18 (NIV) says, "The LORD is close to the brokenhearted and saves those who are crushed in spirit."

I had invited God to be with me and help me through this heartbreaking experience. I felt the benefit of God's presence and invited Him into the waiting room to wait the long wait with me…to talk me through a scary time. What I did not know is that I would meet with the Creator of Heaven and Earth face to face that night. I felt His presence all around me. I clung to it. God reached down to comfort me and sit with me in my pain.

I found myself looking around not knowing where I was. I looked up to see a nurse who was wheeling me on a stretcher from the operating room to the recovery area. She looked into my eyes and spoke softly. She reminded me about my beautiful daughter at home. She shared it once and then again: "Everything will be okay."

But that's what I had wanted to hear all those other times during the last 24 hours!

And yet now the words came accompanied by the heartbreak of the loss of our baby. In some way, they offered a peace beyond what I could understand. I had an assurance in some way that even though I would go home and grieve this tremendous loss, everything would be okay.

When terrible things happen, we have some choices. One option is to run to God. And one, which I think is common and understandable, is that we can get really angry at God. Another is that we can run away from Him and question, "How could you let this happen, God?"

Shortly after, I remember my husband speaking with someone who had a similar heartbreaking experience. They confided in him that they were mad at God and turned their back on Him. I could connect with their pain and hard place. This was a significant time in my faith journey. A crisis of belief is something I can relate to and wrestled with. But what I found in those fearful moments as it felt like my heart was being pulled out of my chest is a peace beyond understanding.

My one-on-one chats with God in the waiting room,
What seemed like a number of face-to-face conversations,
A warm, comforting embrace,
And the long-awaited words that everything would be okay—
Met me in this painful and hard place.

This painful circumstance cemented something in me—a firmer foundation of sorts. A new "God and me kind of thing" and a greater commitment to surrender and run to Him in the good and terrible times. This personal face-to-face encounter with a personal, loving, and caring God established this immovable faith in me—

This "I trust you, Lord, whatever happens."

"I'm running to you, Lord, in this painful situation and the next one."

A hard place. How do we reconcile great losses and suffering in our lives? It's not fair! Why do these difficulties need to happen? What about the loss? What about the unbelievable pain?

There are times when we just don't have the answers. We may or may not be aware that God is working behind the scenes for our good. Either way, it's overwhelmingly painful when you are in the middle of a crisis.

The Bible says, "And we know that in all things God works for the good of those who love him, who have been called according to his purpose." (Romans 8:28 NIV)

Would we be courageous and invite Jesus to lovingly hold us and sit with us in our pain even when we don't understand what's happening?

I believe one day we will meet Jesus face to face, and He will wipe every tear away from our eyes. It's then when we will see the "big picture story" that God is painting. The Bible assures us that "He will wipe every tear from their eyes, and there will be no more death or sorrow or crying or pain. All these things are gone forever" (Revelation 21:4 NLT).

I remember reading a poem written by a child whose dear mom had a miscarriage before she was pregnant for them. The child in the poem thanked her for the courage to try again, and as a result, they came into this world. Our second child, our son, was born seven months after our lost baby would have been born. I can't imagine my life without our sweet boy. He's brought to our family a warm, loving embrace (he gives the best hugs!) and an abundance of love and joy that's been heaven sent.

There are so many questions that we don't have the answers to on this side of heaven. What we know is God promises to be with us in our pain and to never leave us there. The enemy would like you to think that God has deserted you in your suffering, but this is not true. To combat this lie, we need to focus on the truth of God's Word and His character toward us, which is truthful, loving, faithful, merciful, just, and kind.

You can run to God, or you can run away from Him. This is the place where you decide who you will trust and what you believe. Heartbreaking times can shake you down to your core. It's how we courageously respond that can yield an immovable faith in a Savior who desires to comfort and care for you in the midst of your pain.

YOUR SACRED TIME, SPACE, AND CALLING

15-MINUTE FREEDOM EXERCISE

I often say, "My faith and two-way conversations with God are how I live and breathe." This statement may be a something you connect with, or it may be completely foreign to you. This "face-to-face" story I shared may have offered hope and encouragement to you, and it could possibly have even stirred up some feelings inside that you are not sure what to do with. There is something I find helpful and do on a regular basis in my journal time. Like the SOAP Bible Study Method, it's something I have in my devotional (quiet time) toolbox that I can draw on from time to time.

Often when I journal, I like to set aside fifteen minutes. When I have negative feelings that are sticking with me, I find it helpful to write at the top of my journal page a question—something like "God, what would you like to say to me through this negative emotion I'm feeling right now? (It's helpful to state the feeling and journal about one feeling at a time.) Or what burden am I carrying that I am not meant to carry in this overwhelming situation? Or what lies am I believing about this situation (or in a relationship or personally about myself)? Or what truth or encouragement do you want to say to me, Lord, about my struggle?"

You may be thinking you'd like to ask God all these questions. Or you may be asking, "Can I really ask God questions like this?" Or you may have some of your own questions you would like to ask. I find it helpful to pick one question at a time and take some time to pause and reflect and then write down the thoughts that come to mind, remembering that God's thoughts and words are not condemning or accusing but convicting, helpful, loving, and kind. If I'm finding it hard to focus, I pray and ask God to deal with the distractions and help me hear His voice. It's not that God can't answer all my questions at once—it's that I really don't have the capacity to receive all His answers at once. And so I ask one at a time and wait, listen, and journal what I'm sensing or what is coming to my mind. I often go back and read and reflect on these journal pages, especially if I'm experiencing similar feelings again. I'll share more with you later in the book—specifically some negative feelings I've taken time to journal about and have seen how God has encouraged me through asking Him about them.

SPECIAL TIME WITH GOD

Set aside 15 minutes. Read **PSALM 34** located in the Old Testament. This psalm has been a place where God has met me in my pain and tended to heartbreak in my life. I pray it is encouraging, healing, and comforting to you.

You may consider reading it a second time out loud. Pick one verse that sticks out or connects with you. Apply the SOAP Method.

S – Scripture – Write out the verse you chose. Write it in this space below or in your own journal.

_____

_____

_____

O – Observation – What are one or two facts that you observe from the verse you chose?

_____

_____

_____

A – Application – How can you personally apply this verse to your life?

_____

_____

_____

P – Prayer – Write out a prayer to God related to your reading today. There is no right or wrong way to do this. Prayer is simply talking with God. Think of this as a conversation starter between you and God.

_____

_____

_____

PRAYER AND ENCOURAGEMENT

Life is full of **highs** and **lows**…you are not meant to journey through them alone.

What is an area of your life where you are **doing well**?

_____

_____

What is an area of your life where you are **struggling**?

_____

_____

_____

Pray! I'm sharing these questions with you again because I'd love for you to establish a habit of sharing your highs and lows with God and others on a regular basis. Remember to pray and thank God for your highs. Ask Him for help with your lows.

Take some time in prayer to share your feelings, joys, and pain with God, who is waiting to spend time with you—He hears you, cares for you, and understands what you are experiencing. Ask Him to speak truth and encouragement into your situation.

Sharing your "highs" and "lows" is something you can share in conversation with your loved ones at meals or bedtime and pray together. Have each person share, and then pray a simple prayer together. Thank God for each of your highs, and ask Him for help with each of your lows. Doing this on a regular basis will help you and your family connect on a deeper level in your relationships with each other and with God.

5

LIKE FLASHING LIGHTS

"Faith is taking the first step even when you don't see
the whole staircase."

MARTIN LUTHER KING, JR.

THE LIGHTS WERE dim, and the band played a song I did not know. I felt overwhelmed and uncomfortable inside. Culture shock surrounded me. No choir. No pews. No red hymn books. No familiar church smell. No one who knew my name.

I then saw a woman I recognized from our local bookstore. She smiled and invited me to sit with her. The pastor shared a message, and I remember hearing a few times the word FREEDOM. For some reason, it stood out like flashing lights to me. I do not remember much else he said. I cried a lot. It felt like there were puddles of tears surrounding my feet. I love how the woman I sat with welcomed me and yet gave me space to sit with Jesus in my tears.

Despite my outward emotional response, I started to feel a new sense of peace inside. You know that feeling when you've been looking for something for a long time and then you find it?

Have you ever needed to decide on something, for example, to stay at your current job or look for a new one, which seemed impossible to make? In this case, my husband and I were considering moving to a new church. I found it a difficult choice to make. And so I gladly welcomed this fresh word FREEDOM and how it exposed the confusion that had been circling around the clarity I so desired.

I remember praying inside and saying, "God, is this why you brought me here? For freedom? For freedom I don't know I don't have?"

"What is holding me back?"

"What am I missing? Is there more?"

Here, as I reflected in this space, I could see more clearly now. I found myself a woman who faithfully served God and yet had this growing desire to know Him on a deeper level.

My heart's cry and prayer that night was that I would be open for whatever God had for me. Soon after, my husband and kids visited, and we decided to move to this new faith community. It was a tremendously difficult decision to leave our church, and yet we knew in our hearts this was the right thing to do for our family. God has honored and blessed this decision beyond what we could have ever imagined. I can't wait to share more with you because if you have not experienced such a peace or blessing, I know that God wants this for you too!

I have to tell you, I really had no idea what was to come as we took this leap of faith. The prayer I prayed then and continue to pray is "Lord, do whatever it takes in my life for my freedom and for your glory." Just in case you are thinking of praying this simple, one-line prayer, I have to say it comes with a disclaimer. It's a dangerous prayer and one that can truly transform a life. The power is not in the words; it is in a person named Jesus Christ, who you would be asking to change you from the inside out. When we ask the God of Heaven and Earth, who created all things, to do whatever it takes in our lives, be sure that He will do exactly what we ask. My world has been rocked again and again. It's all good. You will see, as you keep reading, how significant it's been for my family to be a part of the RIGHT faith community for us.

Fast forward a few years—I found myself in a baptism tank! Again, one of those "I did not see this coming" scenarios. Stay with me; it gets better. Here's the testimony I shared with our faith-building and encouraging community:

> *Three years ago, I was in a place where I had a relationship with Jesus, but I so desperately wanted to know Him more. A wife and mom with a three-year-old and a six-month-old at the time, I was tired, overloaded, and unknowingly wounded. I was serving in another church and had just started leading in a ministry. In my condition, I remember asking Jesus, what could I possibly say to this group of people I was going to be meeting with? I sensed Him giving me these words from Matthew 11 verses 28 to 30 to share with them.*
>
> *"Come to me, all you who are weary and burdened, and I will give you rest. Take my yoke upon you and learn from me, for I am gentle and humble in heart, and you will find rest for your souls. For my yoke is easy and my burden is light."*
>
> *That day, this invitation from Jesus penetrated my heart and led me on a new path in a new direction. Looking back now, I really had no idea what was coming. Soon after, Jesus led my family here to this church. He brought people into our lives to journey with us. He brought us to a safe place.*
>
> *Since then, Jesus has led me on a journey of healing and restoration, and it's been during this time that God gave me this promise. It's in Psalm 103:1–5, and it reflects my heart and describes my journey.*
>
> *Praise the LORD, my soul;*
> *all my inmost being, praise His holy name.*
> *Praise the LORD, my soul,*
> *and forget not all His benefits—*

Who forgives all your sins
and heals all your diseases,
Who redeems your life from the pit
and crowns you with love and compassion,
Who satisfies your desires with good things
so that your youth is renewed like the eagle's.

My life has been radically transformed these last three years. I am learn-
ing from Jesus...who He is...and who I am in Him...AND IN HIM,
I am finding rest for my soul. When I look back, I see that God had so
much more for me...and my husband and our kids. I am just so thankful
that we are not missing it. I love you, Lord Jesus. I thank you, and I need
you now more than ever before.

There's a radio station I like to listen to in my car. But sadly, I receive poor reception, resulting in lots of static and frustration in the middle of a talk radio show I'm enjoying. And perhaps, for some people, even more tragic depending on your music taste, there's a country music radio station that cuts in on occasion. Sigh!

I remember the exact day and time when the light bulb went off and I realized I could clearly distinguish the voice of God from the other voices competing for my attention. Like with my radio station dilemma, finally a crystal clear reception and no interruptions! The clarity came with God-given healing, love, truth, and encouragement. It also helped me further discern and reject the voice of the enemy, lies, and deception.

So does God really speak to us? In some ways, He's been speaking to us our whole lives, and for some, like myself, it took me a long time to tune in to His voice. A friend describes it like a telephone where God is calling us and is waiting for us to pick up and answer and have a conversation with Him.

In hearing from God, I thought I'd share some suggestions of how we can gain clarity and test when we are hearing Gods' voice. Here are five questions that have helped me over the years. They are adapted from a Bible study called

What Happens When Women Say Yes to God: Experiencing Life in Extraordinary Ways by Lysa TerKeurst.[1]

1. Does what I'm hearing line up with the Bible?

    "God will never speak to us or tell us to do something that is contrary to Scripture. But unless we know and read the Bible, we will not be able to discern whether what we are hearing is consistent with God's truth." If we lead and mentor people of faith, we have a responsibility to know God's Word and help them discern the truth. A friend of mine is gifted at affirming (or gently not affirming) if something lines up with Scripture. She is further along in her Bible knowledge than I am, and I'm thankful to have her in my life to help me in this area. Jesus says in John 7:17 (NIV), "Anyone who chooses to do the will of God will find out whether my teaching comes from God or whether I speak on my own."

2. Is what I'm hearing consistent with God's character?

    "God's Word also provides rich information regarding His character." As you are intentional about reading the Bible for yourself, you will discover more about who God is and also more about who you are in Him. This equipping is essential in helping you discern if what you are hearing is consistent with God's nature and personality. When you are reading the Bible, take time to highlight, reflect on, and underline God's character traits. James 3:17 (NIV) says, "But the wisdom that comes from heaven is first of all pure; then peace-loving, considerate, submissive, full of mercy and good fruit, impartial and sincere."

3. Is what I'm hearing confirmed through messages at church or my quiet times with God?

    "When God is speaking to me about a particular issue, it's like I cannot escape it. Around every corner there is a sermon, a Bible study lesson, a speaker's topic, or a conversation with a friend that is consistent with what I've been hearing from God in my time alone with Him."

4. Is what I'm hearing beyond me?

"Sometimes God calls us to do something big that we can't do in our own strength; either it is beyond our ability or beyond our human desire." I don't know about you, but I want to be a part of something bigger than myself. I think we all desire to be a part of a greater story.

5. Is what I'm hearing pleasing to God?

"We should always seek to err on the side of pleasing God. Ask this question, and you will know what to do."

Know that God's voice is not condemning but convicting, helpful, loving, and kind. Obsessing, worrisome, discouraging, and confusing thoughts are not of God.
Know that—
God's voice calms you.
God's voice comforts you.
God's voice convicts you.
God's voice encourages you.
God's voice counsels you.
God's voice directs you.
God's voice empowers you.
God's voice forgives you.
God's voice equips you.
God's voice reassures you.
God's voice blesses you.
God's voice quiets you with His love.
God's voice sings over you with joy.

"For the LORD your God is living among you. He is a mighty savior. He will take delight in you with gladness. With his love, he will calm all your fears. He will rejoice over you with joyful songs." (Zephaniah 3:17 NLT)

I'm so glad God changed my perspective that night and how the word FREEDOM captured my attention. I'm incredibly thankful He removed the blinders from my eyes and made it obvious to me. Wow, and to think I could have missed something I didn't have. Can you relate in any way to my new-found understanding? Has God ever interrupted your thinking? Would you like Him to?

I hope you are encouraged as I share my story and are inspired to look at your own story and share with others. My freedom journey has very much been a process and a series of next steps that continue to unfold in becoming a Freedom Fighter and Truth Teller.

Becoming a Freedom Fighter & Truth Teller by Kim Gowdy
You could call me the worst kind of captive.
I did not know I was not free.
On the overwhelmed road, there's no margin.
Tiredness. Burnout. In need of rest and healing.
Where does one find hope for the weary?
How did I let my plate get this full?
Where is there any room for the longings in my heart?

Thankful to have found this FREEDOM road,
Where I've found rest and healing in truly knowing Jesus.
I'm a faith-filled work in process.
Meeting on this road—Truth, Love, Grace, and Mercy along the way.
It's not that the burdens are not there anymore.
Just that they are lighter and easier when I surrender them to my Savior.

Freedom is not free. There's a cost—a sacrifice.
It's a satisfying and life-giving process that is worth it to pursue.
A Freedom Fighter and Truth Teller is WHO I'm called to be.
Freedom is worth standing and fighting for—
For the eternal value and reward is priceless.

What is something you are longing for? Maybe you don't have a relationship with God or, like me, you desire a deeper, more intimate connection with Him. I'm glad you are here. Stay with me as I share more. It's a path and journey that is worth taking the next step in front of you. God will meet you where you are and clear a path for more freedom in your life. He's going before you, beside you, and all around you. Keep going. Don't miss it. Be open to what He has for you.

YOUR SACRED TIME, SPACE, AND CALLING

15-MINUTE FREEDOM EXERCISE

"If I find in myself a desire which no experience in this world can satisfy, the most probable explanation is that I was made for another world."[2]
C.S. Lewis

What are some flashing lights for you? Do you have a desire for more? More rest, more healing, or more FREEDOM? What do you want? What is something you desire for your life? I'd love for you to take some time to reflect on these questions. What's on your heart as you read this? Write whatever comes to your mind. Be creative as you think about the possibilities. Just write. Suspend the judge inside of you. You can use the space provided or use your own journal to write as much as you like. The more, the better.

Personally, I wanted a deeper relationship with God. Maybe this is not something you are thinking about. I also wanted to be free from the burdens I didn't know I could be free from or even how they were holding me back.

As I gained more clarity, I felt confident I needed to keep journeying back to God and His purposes for me.

Remember, freedom is a process. Be kind to yourself along the way. I pray for God's wisdom and clarity for you. I pray God brings people to come alongside you and speak truth and love into your life. I pray for a passion in you to fight for the freedom God has for you and the people you care about.

Take some time to **Free(dom) Write**.

_____

_____

_____

_____

_____

_____

_____

_____

_____

_____

_____

_____

_____

_____

_____

SPECIAL TIME WITH GOD

Set aside 15 minutes. Read **PSALM 18** in the Old Testament. You may consider reading it a second time out loud. What verse sticks out or connects with you? Apply the SOAP Method.

S – Scripture – Write out the verse you chose. Write it in this space below or in your journal.

_____

_____

_____

O – Observation – What are one or two facts that you observe from the verse you chose?

_____

_____

_____

A – Application – How can you personally apply this verse to your life?

_____

_____

_____

P – Prayer – Write out a prayer to God related to your reading today. There is no right or wrong way to do this. Prayer is having a conversation with God. Think of this as a conversation starter between you and God.

_____

_____

_____

PRAYER AND ENCOURAGEMENT

Would you be willing to pray this prayer?

Pray! Lord God my Savior, I give you my life. I give you my heavy burdens. Forgive me of my sins—the sins I know about and the ones I don't know about. Please, Holy Spirit, come into my life, move freely, and fill me with your priorities and agenda for my life. God, please do whatever it takes—CHANGE ME FROM THE INSIDE OUT—for my Freedom and for your Glory. Bring me back to you, Lord, and Your purposes for my life. Your Kingdom come and your will be done here on earth as it is in heaven. Help me get off this Overwhelmed Road and on to the FREEDOM Road that you have for me. Help me become a Freedom Fighter and a Truth Teller who loves people and, most of all, loves you, Lord. Help me to be the person you created me to be. Help me share my freedom story with others so they can see you through me and be changed as well. In Your precious and powerful name, Jesus, Amen.

PART II—UNLOCKED

"The caged bird sings with a fearful trill,
of things unknown, but longed for still,
and his tune is heard on the distant hill,
for the caged bird sings of freedom."

MAYA ANGELOU, *I KNOW WHY THE CAGED BIRD SINGS*

JUST BECAUSE A cage is unlocked does not mean we are free. Some may decide to stay trapped inside because it is familiar to us. Whether we stay in the cage with what we know or fly out to the unknown, it takes a decision. It's a choice to stay or to go. It's a defining moment where we know that we are going to do this—and leave this stuck place.

We are then faced with a series of decisions to take action and break free. It's being willing to admit where we are on the journey, owning and telling our story, asking for help, doing the hard work, and breaking free.

6

BREAKING THE CYCLE

"Between every unfaithful generation and faithful generation is
one person determined to change. You could be that link. So could
I. Perhaps no one in your family was overtly sinful, but they were
simply uninvolved in Christ's kingdom. Maybe you would like to be
a link that takes your family line from an unfulfilling life of religion
to a passionate life of relationship with Christ."

BETH MOORE, *BREAKING FREE: DISCOVER THE VICTORY OF TOTAL SURRENDER*

I NOTICED THE WORKSHOP listed on the conference schedule and quickly
skipped over it. It felt like something inside me breathed a sigh of relief.
Okay, let's stick to why I am here on this rare kid-free day.
So why am I here?
God, PLEASE give me parenting wisdom had been my daily prayer, and
I felt this conference was an answer in some way. But really, deep down

underneath, I desperately needed to be rescued from the overwhelming feelings inside that were coming to the surface and would no longer stay down.

Here's a workshop on personality types. This looks like a good one. I found these types of assessments quite useful in my previous corporate job when working in a team environment.

I then saw my friend walking towards me—she had been looking at the workshop options as well. Enthusiastically, she shared "I'm going to *Breaking the Cycle of Hurt* led by Dr. Merry Lin. Will you join me?"

"Umm. I just heard that one is full—I'm actually looking at a different one over here."

Yet I could tell from her facial expression she wasn't going to take no for an answer, and she convincingly exclaimed, "Let's go! It's going to be a good one."

It looked like every chair had been taken until we noticed two empty seats on the other side of the room. "Come in, we are about to start the workshop," greeted the presenter.

Oh my goodness, how could I graciously escape this presentation and, more specifically, the physical response rising up inside of me to it? And then I found myself sitting down, and if it could get any worse, we were sitting in the FRONT ROW!

I found the speaker's gentle approach both encouraging and calming. It helped me settle in to hear the presentation. Trained in psychology, she addressed a topic I didn't know a great deal about. I started to find myself in the stories she shared, and it intrigued me enough to switch gears into learning mode while ignoring the stirred up feelings inside.

She talked about our family of origin, how we can't live with them and we can't live without them. This was something I could relate to, and although my family lived far away, the feelings and hurt continued to find me despite the distance.

I learned more about attachment parenting, something my husband and I had desired for our kids, as well as behavioral styles and how we respond to the world, which is greatly determined when we are babies and by how we are parented in the first twelve months of our lives. As relationship styles were described, I felt like I saw my life flash before me as I thought of the unhealthy relationships, negative emotions, hurt, and pain that I had experienced in my life.

Looking back at the first year of my life, my parents met at a Baptist Bible school, and I was conceived outside of marriage. My parents were then married shortly after I was born. While my mom worked and went to school, I had been cared for by other family and non-family caregivers and saw my mom on weekends and sometimes not for longer periods of time until she finished school.

We then moved to live with my dad, who had been working and building a home for us. My parents, I think, tried to protect me and didn't share these timeline details until I found out when I was a young girl. From that point on, I had the impression that I had been a mistake and my parents would have not been married had it not been for me. This heavy burden in some way attached itself to my shoulders and yielded inside of me feelings of unworthiness, guilt, and shame. This combined with growing up in a home where on the outside, efforts were focused on what others thought—but on the inside, emotional, physical, and spiritual needs were not always considered and heart damage occurred. All this taking its toll, my coping mechanisms became that of a people-pleaser and the glue that enabled others and kept everyone together.

Back to the parenting workshop…as I sat in this front row conference chair, I thought about how I felt like the wheels were falling off the bus for me—one wheel at a time. Taking inventory of my situation, I found myself overcommitted, overreacting, and not equipped to respond to the negative emotions coming to the surface in my own home and family life.

I loved and adored my husband and kids, and yet they were the ones who seemed to trigger and stir up these negative feelings that were coming to the surface. They were on the receiving end of my coming unglued in response to past and ongoing hurt by others. Hurt people tend to hurt people. This is what I experienced in the past, and now I was responding in an unhealthy way out of my own hurt. As much as I desired to be different, I could not give what I did not have, nor did I have the capacity or the understanding to respond in a healthier way.

Why was this all coming to the surface now? Could I have not figured all this out prior to getting married and having children? What had I missed? Could these negative feelings not just go away so that we could get on with the pain-free, loving relationships that I so desired?

And then I heard the speaker say that no matter the choices I make in parenting my children, if I did not learn how to have healthy relationships, if I did not deal with my stuff, my messes, my hurts, my wounds—I would pass all of this on to my children, and THEY would carry my pain.

Oh my goodness. It's a repeating cycle! The pain gets passed on from parent to child, from parent to child, and so on.

What? You mean the pain that I can't take any more and I want to stop, I am passing it on to my kids? My kids carry MY pain?

No, not my kids!

How did I miss this?

And then I heard the speaker share this quote by Peter Colliers that sounded all too familiar—

"Sometimes you'll get so far away from your family you'll think you're outside its influence forever, then before you figure out what's happening, it will be right beside you, pulling the strings."[1]

The presentation was over, and my friend encouragingly insisted, "Let's go ask the speaker a question!" As if my "deer in the headlights" look was not enough of a deterrent, she went on to share that it was really worth asking a question based on how much she charges an hour for therapy.

Now standing in line, I thought, what would I ask? I honestly had no idea. And then four words came out of my mouth—

"Can one person change?"

What?! Did I really say that?

"I mean—can one person change and make a difference if everything around them stays the same?"

I then shared a bit of my story, and her response was yes. She went on to explain the importance of going to a professional counselor to help identify core pain issues, areas of wounding, and next steps towards healing.

I felt like my world had just been shaken up like a snow globe. Something inside of me told me I needed to keep moving in this direction. The resistance inside directed towards attending this workshop was now being exposed.

I bought a book on the recommended list called *Why You Do the Things You Do: The Secret to Healthy Relationships* by Tim Clinton and Gary Sibcy. As I read, I gained greater awareness and discovered more about the hope and healing available. When I finished the book, I literally picked up the phone and called a Christian counseling center and officially made the decision to Break the Cycle of Hurt.

My same dear friend reminded me more recently that I would say I went to counseling for my kids. This is most definitely true. My dear precious children are how God got my attention, and I am incredibly thankful.

I have to tell you I did wrestle with one thing. You see, there were people in my life who I thought needed to go for counseling more than I did. I found myself making excuses why I didn't need to go. But my situation as a parent was different than my parents—my kids were with me, and by the grace of God, my husband and I were on the same page and had similar attachment parenting styles.

Then I realized my situation was not completely different. Yes, I was physically present for my kids, but my presence came with an inherited addiction, which I would later learn is called codependency. Was I really present? Was I really available to my kids? And what about not being able to give what I did not have—remembering my wheels falling off the bus and my love tank on empty.

What is codependency? I've learned it is something passed down from parents to children. My counselor recommended a book called *Love Is a Choice: The Definitive Book on Letting Go of Unhealthy Relationships* by Robert Hemfelt, which opened my eyes to the tendencies that had been passed on to me. I learned codependency is common in North America, where they say one in four people suffer from it. Simply defined, it is when a person has a need to control another person in a relationship or they have a feeling of lack of control in a relationship. This sure resonated in my experience in relationships. How about you?

For me personally, people pleasing and the underlying need to fix or keep everything together in my family of origin and other relationships pointed to my own codependent tendencies that God now wanted to bring to the light and heal.

The bottom line was that I personally needed counseling. No excuses. And so I say I went with Jesus for counseling for three years—the first two years I had an appointment once a week. I didn't know how long I'd be going. I took it one week at a time and sensed that I was to keep going. Sometimes I didn't know what I'd talk with my counselor about, and I remember driving to appointments asking God and His Spirit to give me the words to say. He did.

God went before me.

God went beside me.

God went all around me.

God brought Freedom Fighters and Truth Tellers into my life. My counselor was a good fit for me. My husband was incredibly supportive. I could not have done this alone. I needed community. I had people at our church who encouraged and prayed for me and my family. God brought to us a beautiful woman of faith who cared for our children for every single counseling appointment. Friends would ask, "What's next for you on your journey?" God made me aware of the voices to listen to and the voices not to listen to.

I sensed God whispering to me—

Let me love you, Kim.

Let me protect you.

Trust me.

You don't need to figure this all out.

Trust me in this moment.

This is ONE step.

One baby step.

Keep going.

My simple but heartfelt prayers—
God, I'm open and do not want to miss anything that you have for me.
Lord, FREE ME TO LOVE.
Lord, do whatever it takes in me for my freedom and for your glory.

As I went through the counseling process, I learned how to set boundaries and work towards healthy relationships. I so needed this process. I learned to separate my stuff from other people's stuff. I learned to guard my heart, to speak the truth in love, and to say no (not exactly something a people pleaser thinks about).

My counselor referred me to a program at our church called Breakthrough, which is a biblically-based, 12-week program in a small and large group setting. Group therapy offered a different type of healing than one-on-one counseling. I needed both. I remember in my small group each week we were asked to identify how we were feeling after the session. I remember thinking I really did not know. The feelings came. I had emotional wounds that God wanted to heal. When I look back at these open wounds and the lies attached to them, they were holding me back from having the relationship with Jesus and others I so desired. As God revealed each lie to me, He revealed His healing truth as well. The process healed my heart inside and made me whole again.

I was changing.

Being renewed.

Being transformed.

Becoming more the person God created me to be.

I was different.

My kids were different.

My daughter, from the time she was a baby, had not been exceedingly affectionate. As I changed, she changed. I love that at eight years old she would she say, "You never get enough hugs from your parents," and "You know, Mommy, I have high hug needs." I could see my husband experiencing his own journey of freedom and how God was moving authentically in his life as well.

My counselor referred me to a prayer ministry at our church to pray through some childhood trauma I had experienced. It was then, through reading recommended books such as *The Bondage Breaker* by Neil T. Anderson, that I learned and became aware that sins of past generations, my family, and my own sins had opened doors to the enemy in my life. I sincerely confessed and turned from these sins. Jesus fought on my behalf and set me free from the oppression and captivity that I didn't know were a part of me. This was something ONLY God could do. When I look back, I remember Him being gentle, kind, merciful, and loving during this healing process. I'm forever grateful.

There've been many layers to my healing, which continues on to this day. My freedom story has been a work in progress, where God has so graciously given me glimpses of hope and much healing along the way.

Miracle after miracle.

Knowing that God is for me and not against me has made all the difference.

Knowing that Jesus is who He says He is has secured my faith and destiny.

Knowing that I am His and He is mine—significant, secure, and accepted in Him—has rewritten my identity.

Knowing that He has a unique plan and purpose for my life has given me a new song to sing.

Knowing I'm anchored in His love has given me a place to go when I am on empty—to the only One who can fill my love tank and give me rest for my soul.

The last few years I've been on a journey of learning more about WHO and WHY I was created to be—I knew at the beginning of my decision to "Break the Cycle of Hurt" that there was hope and healing available. What I did not know is that on the other side would be a dream, a renewed passion, and a vision God had for my life. I can't wait to share with you more about my BIG DREAM in another chapter.

For now, let me end this story with the question I reluctantly asked in the beginning: "Can one person change and make a difference if everything around them stays the same?" And with overwhelming gratitude, I'm thankful to say, now with enthusiasm,

"Yes, I am a living testimony that one person can change!"

I am truly thankful to be taking proactive steps in helping my kids not carry my pain. A decision to Break the Cycle of Hurt is not a one-time event—it's a decision I need to make every day. It's a decision that can bring more pain, but it is a pain that is accompanied by purpose and healing. It's a decision through which I've seen myself and my loved ones redeemed and set free. It's a decision that has changed the paths and destinies of my beloved family and future generations. It's a decision through which I don't ever want to forget to remember what God has done. I share this truth and encouragement from God's Word with you—

"Let the redeemed of the LORD tell their story—those he redeemed from the hand of the foe," (Psalm 107:2 NIV)

"So each generation should set its hope anew on God, not forgetting his glorious miracles and obeying his commands. Then they will not be like their ancestors—stubborn, rebellious, and unfaithful, refusing to give their hearts to God." (Psalm 78:7–8 NLT)

YOUR SACRED TIME, SPACE, AND CALLING

15-MINUTE FREEDOM EXERCISE

How do you tell your story? How do you find your voice? How can you share your story in a way that is honoring to everyone, including yourself? I think the first step is taking some time to write out your story. It doesn't need to be perfect—simply write what comes to mind, and try to suspend any internal criticism. You can go back later, review, and make changes. For now, you want to release your story from your head to the page.

I personally find there is something that happens when you put pen to paper (or fingers to a keyboard), especially when you are feeling stuck. I like to say, "Give me a journal, and I will fill it up." I've found journaling is—

- An encouraging, healing, and effective way to find your voice.
- A powerful way to tell your story.
- A potential legacy piece for future generations to read.
- Beneficial for a closer relationship with God as you engage in an honest and unpretending conversation with Him.
- Helpful for getting you unstuck.

Set aside 15 minutes. Start by taking some time to **Free(dom) Write** (which I like to define as free writing without editing in a physical or computer journal). Write out your story. Don't edit. If you are not sure what to write, put down "I don't know what to write." Keep setting aside time to write out your story. If you are like me, you'll find this can be a healing process, and it can also bring feelings, thoughts, or wounds to mind that may need further attention, restoration, and healing. Be sure to take some time to pray, asking God for wisdom and the next steps for you on your journey. Ask someone to pray with or for you if you need further clarity.

SPECIAL TIME WITH GOD
Set aside 15 minutes. Psalm 103:1–5 is a promise I sensed from God early in making the decision to Break the Cycle of Hurt. It's something I go back to, especially in times when I'm feeling discouraged, and for me personally, it breathes new hope into my sails. I pray your special time with God in His Word is life-giving and an encouragement to you.

Read **PSALM 103** in the Old Testament. Read it a second time out loud. What verse in this scripture passage stands out or connects with you? Apply the SOAP Method.

S – Scripture – Write out the verse you chose. Write it in this space below or in your journal.

_____

_____

_____

O – Observation – What are one or two facts that you observe from the verse you chose?

_____

_____

_____

A – Application – How can you personally apply this verse to your life?

_____

_____

_____

P – Prayer – Write out a prayer to God related to your reading today. There is no right or wrong way to do this. Prayer is having a conversation with God. Think of this as a conversation starter between you and God.

_____

_____

_____

PRAYER AND ENCOURAGEMENT

Sometimes we just need to **turn down** the **noise**.

Take five minutes to listen to what God is saying to you in this moment. Write down the thoughts that come to mind here or in your own journal. It's okay if you don't sense anything to start. It takes time and practice to hear God's voice. Jesus affirms to us in John 10:27 (NIV), "My **sheep** listen to **my voice**; I know them, and they follow me." What thoughts or encouragement do you sense God impressing on you? Go back to this encouragement when you are struggling. God speaks to us in truth and love. If we are sensing something other than this, we can be assured it is not from Him. Ask God to help you tune out the discouragement and tune in to the life-giving words He has for you.

_____

_____

_____

_____

_____

_____

_____

Pray! Ask God to help you hear His voice and to hear it clearly. Here is a prayer I wrote in my journal around the time I felt called to write this book. I hope it is an encouragement to you.

Lord God my Savior, Lord Jesus, You are calling me to write. Thank you for the clarity you are providing. Thank you for the people you are bringing into my life. You say you are all I need to do this. You are all I need to connect people to you. Thank you for the privilege to partner with you. Thank you for trusting me with the story you have given me. Thank you for the refining work you are doing in my life. Thank you for the struggles you have placed in my story and the character you are growing in me. It is my desire to honor you in all that I do. Please Lord, completely purify my motives. I give you my dreams, my hopes, my failures and my successes, and the gifts and abilities you have given me. I do not want to hold on to the results of what this will all look like. I give it all to you. You know what I need. You know what I need to do. I trust you, Lord. I am staying grounded in what you are telling me and asking me to do. I love you, Lord.

7

NEED TO KNOW

"The past does not have to be your prison. You have a voice in your destiny. You have a say in your life. You have a choice in the path you take."

MAX LUCADO, *WHEN GOD WHISPERS YOUR NAME*

I HAVE A confession. I'm a crier. Basically, I cry when I'm happy, sad, and anywhere in between. As someone who has a heart to pray for others, there are times when my tears are not my own and represent those who cannot pray. Not on this day a year ago, however. These tears were triggered by hurt and broken trust and came like uninvited guests for the weekend.

As I stood in the kitchen emptying the dishwasher, I noticed one tear streaming down one side of my face. For three days they came one after another. Not the uncontrollable kind but a constant streaming flow. My tears in some way were helping the pain inside come out. They gave me assurance that I'm not alone and God is with me.

The Bible assures us, "You keep track of all my sorrows. You have collected all my tears in your bottle. You have recorded each one in your book." (Psalm 56:8 NLT)

Thankfully, tears are a way my Creator encourages, heals, and cleanses me. When I get hurt emotionally and have no words, graciously, my tears step in and become my prayers.

They help me grieve, and they give me hope.

They help me feel and communicate my love for others and my passions in life.

They tell me my God is good.

They've helped me write this book and be real and authentic with you.

My tears are part of who I am and my calling in life—not wasted but purposeful—and serve as a ministry of tears of sorts. I'm okay with it.

When the tears come, I try not to push them away and instead be present with them. Sometimes I remember to ask God, "Why the tears?" and learn more about their meaning and what's behind them. There's a peace and a maturity that comes with them now, and I know I'm okay and they are part of me.

They say time heals all wounds. I don't think this is the case. What if I have an emotional wound that appears to be healed on the surface and unknowingly is festering underneath?

We may have past or present hurts that have not been healed and are in need of some attention. Instead, we are not aware and stuff, ignore, numb, or hide our pain arising from the hurts. The problem with this strategy is it does not give our pain a voice, nothing gets resolved, and the hurt continues. As I've shared, hurt people tend to hurt people. And either knowingly or unknowingly, the people we care about are impacted the most; as I've learned through counseling, we can pass on our unresolved pain to our children to carry.

It doesn't have to be this way. There is hope.

What if we were willing to take steps to overcome our hurts?

What if we were willing to have a conversation?

It's been said that the area of our deepest pain and struggle could potentially be the place where we have the greatest impact and influence in the world around us. When I'm preoccupied with pain caused in my relationships or circumstances, it's hard to see the purpose in my pain or how it can help me understand my mission and calling in life.

What if the hurt continues?

What if the person who hurts you continues to do so or they are not willing to accept responsibility or change themselves?

You may need to consider seeking help for yourself and setting healthy boundaries with this person if necessary. Go for counseling if needed. Make peace with God. Ask Him for wisdom and direction regarding your next steps. Let God know how you are feeling. It's okay to say, "God! I'm SO sad, depressed, discouraged, and angry about this!"

"Jesus said to the people who believed in him, 'You are truly my disciples if you remain faithful to my teachings. And you will know the truth, and the truth will set you free.'" (John 8:31–32 NLT)

The fact is, you need to know the truth for it to set you free.

Ultimately, healing and freedom come from God in His timing and through the finished work of Jesus. I think God honors our choices and desires whether they are "for transformation and freedom" or to "stay stuck where we are and not change."

When I started writing this book, my hope was to share my faith journey and how I'm Breaking the Cycle of Hurt in my life—and then I got hurt again. And so I find myself going through some of same "next steps" that I intended to share with you and discovering again how "when I get HURT, I NEED to KNOW how to GO FREE."

Thankfully, when we've gone through something the first time, it's easier the second and third time. Not that we want to get hurt. Maybe a more preferred example is when you've written your first book; you know how to do it, and it's easier to write your second and third book. My hope is that by sharing my story and experiences, it will encourage you to look at your story and share yours.

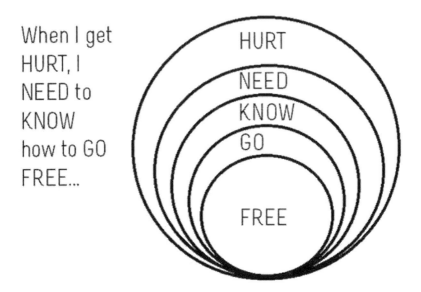

When I get HURT, I NEED to KNOW how to GO FREE...

HURT
NEED
KNOW
GO
FREE

<u>When I get HURT, I NEED to KNOW how to GO FREE.</u>

1. HURT—What is really going on?

    When I'm feeling overwhelmed, my stomach is the first place my stress goes. It's a warning sign that I need to pay attention to and take care of myself or it will get worse.

    I found myself in this position a year ago. I went to the health food store to see if they had any suggestions for my upset tummy. The store clerk had helped me before, and I felt comfortable sharing what had been happening. "I've been under some crazy stress and have experienced some emotional hurts and my stomach is not responding well at all." As she thought about what to suggest, she paused and inquired, "Do you want to treat the symptom or the root of the problem?"

    "Good question!" I responded out loud and then thought to myself how significant treating the root of the problem is to me. I knew full well the pain I was experiencing was just the tip of the iceberg, and I needed to know more about the emotional hurt underneath.

She gave me a suggestion of an effective supplement to support and help my body respond to the extra stress. I later met my doctor, who gave me some simple food suggestions that have helped me even more. I also knew, based on past experiences, I needed to address not just physical healing but emotional and spiritual healing as well.

When I decided to Break the Cycle of Hurt, I knew it would be a choice I'd need to keep on making. God has given me a heart and a passion to fight for and pursue freedom and wholeness for myself and my family. The good news is that as we become more aware of what keeps our hearts from being whole, we discover there is hope and healing available as we go down this Freedom Road.

Emotional hurts break our hearts into pieces. We do not have control over it. We can build walls around our hearts to protect ourselves. We can say something like "I will never let them hurt me again!" or "I will never put myself it that situation again!" First of all, it's not okay when people hurt us or when bad things happen. Sometimes it's not what's been done to us but what's not been done to care for our hearts. It's our response to the hurt that we are responsible for that can potentially get us in some trouble. The problem is when we make a vow and say we will never do something; often what ends up happening is exactly what we declared would not happen. The problem is we make these agreements in our strength and not God's strength. We take matters into our own hands instead of seeking His help when needed. I often say to my kids, "Don't say never; instead, ask God for help in the situation."

Think about it—have you made any vows in your life? Have you had this happen where you said you will never do something or you'll never be like someone and this is exactly what ends up happening? Pray and break these agreements now. Ask God to help you.

We need our hearts to be healed and made whole again. New hurts are often connected to wounds from our past. Often hurts happen to us when we are young, and it affects how we respond in relationships and how we see the world around us. When I received awareness and experienced freedom and healing from childhood hurts, I began to see life differently and genuinely desire this same freedom for the people I care about. I no longer wanted God to fix the people who hurt me but for them to experience the God-given freedom He so graciously offers to them as well.

2. NEED—What do you want?

When I think about this question in the context of being hurt by someone or a circumstance in my life, I think about how I just want the pain to go away. Make it stop! I just want something or someone to take the pain away and fix my problem. In the past, I had wanted God to fix the person or change the circumstance that hurt me.

A friend just posted this quote by Henry Nouwen on her social media page. "The great temptation is to keep blaming those who were closest to us for our present condition saying: 'You made me who I am now, and I hate who I am.' The great challenge is to acknowledge our hurts and claim our true selves as being more than the result of what other people do to us. Only when we can claim our God-made selves as the true source of our being will we be free to forgive those who have wounded us."

Ouch! This reminds me of some of the pity parities I used to host.

My coach says, "Want to FEEL different? Then you need to BE different. The SECRET is simple. You don't get WHAT you want; you get WHO you are. Don't focus on changing your CIRCUMSTANCES; focus on changing YOURSELF. Most people 'are anxious to improve their circumstances, but are unwilling to improve themselves; therefore they remain bound.' —James Allen"[1]

Do you want to heal from your hurts? Would you like to see the areas where you've felt voiceless, caged, trapped, in a mess, and overwhelmed resolved in your life? Would you like to be free? You have to make the decision. No one can do this for you.

Is it a need or is it a want? I want to be free. What I think every human needs is to feel loved, accepted, valued, significant, secure, and a sense that they belong and are safe. Where does one find this? At the drugstore? The doctor's office? Well, maybe a different kind of Doctor—the one I'm thinking of, His name is Jesus.

The Bible tells us, "When Jesus heard this, he told them, 'Healthy people don't need a doctor—sick people do. I have come to call not those who think they are righteous, but those who know they are sinners.'" (Mark 2:17 NLT)

I've shared that this book is not a self-help book but a God-helps book. Asking God to meet me in my hurt and help me get emotionally, physically, and spiritually well has made all the difference.

"Hundreds of sick people—blind, crippled, paralyzed—were in these alcoves. One man had been an invalid there for thirty-eight years. When Jesus saw him stretched out by the pool and knew how long he had been there, he said, 'Do you want to get well?' The sick man said, 'Sir, when the water is stirred, I don't have anybody to put me in the pool. By the time I get there, somebody else is already in.' Jesus said, 'Get up, take your bedroll, start walking.' The man was healed on the spot. He picked up his bedroll and walked off." (John 5:3–8 The Message) Note: Here I'm quoting The Message, which opposed to a biblical translation, is a paraphrase of the Bible written by Eugene Peterson.

3. KNOW—What are the possibilities?
When you feel trapped, caged, and overwhelmed, you feel like you have no options.

Know that the truth gives you options. Know that with freedom, you have choices. You have the option to go from—

No truth to Truth.
No hope to Hope.
No choice to Choice.
No voice to Voice.
No love to Love.
No peace to Peace.
No destiny to Destiny.

No community to Community.
No help to Help.
No power to Power.
No healing to Healing.
No victory to Victory.
No freedom to Freedom.
No calling to Calling.
No blessing to Blessing.
No legacy to Lasting Legacy.

"Now the Lord is the Spirit, and where the Spirit of the Lord is, there is freedom." (2 Corinthians 3:17 NIV)

4. GO—What is the next step?
   First things first, you've got to choose to become a Freedom Fighter. There's a quote I've seen on social media a number of times. It goes something like this: "I want to be the type of person who when I wake up in the morning, the devil says, 'Oh no, she's up!'" You need to be that person! If you feel like you don't have any fight left in you, ask God to help you. The victory has been won by Jesus Christ—He's fought the ultimate battle on your behalf and made a way for your freedom. A Christine Caine quote says, "We don't fight for victory; we fight from victory."[2]

   Secondly, you need to choose to be a Truth Teller. If you are an un-diagnosed people pleaser like I was, you may find this to be a challenge. I know it wrecked me. But if God can equip me to speak the truth in love to others, you have it made in the shade. Just be open and on the lookout for opportunities or God appointments to practice. You're on your way! I'm excited for you.

   Let's get right into some practical next steps. I'd like to share what has helped me. *This is not me saying you need to do exactly what I did.* I believe people are healed and achieve freedom and wholeness in different ways. But just in case you are wondering, here's how I've overcome some of my struggles. I'm happy to share my journey, and I hope that you find this encouraging and helpful.

- It starts with Jesus. Do you have a personal relationship with Him? Have you asked Jesus to be your Lord and Savior? Remember, this is a God-helps book and not a self-help book. I've tried it my own way and had to come to the absolute end of myself before I found my way back to God. I hope I can save you some time. What do you have to lose?
- These next steps are not in a particular order. Read them and see if any resonate with you. I'd like to say I had this big grand plan I followed, but really, my freedom journey has resembled a series of me taking the "next step" in front of me—often in faith, trusting God and taking one small step at a time. It's imperative to remember to "GO towards God!" And keep going. Keep journeying back to Him and WHO He created you to be.
- I can't say enough how crucial it is to ask God for help. Ask others for help. This can be hard to do. Personally, I didn't really know I could or how to do this, but when I did, it was a game changer, and I saw transformation in my life come much faster.
- Reach out to a local faith community where you can connect, heal, and grow. Be a part of a local church that values and meets the physical, emotional, and spiritual needs of its members. Reach out for extra help and support from a good counselor (Christian if possible but not necessary), pastor, coach, small group, etc. Get the help you need. Make the appointment. If you have a spouse or family member who is not willing to resolve issues or go for counseling, consider going on your own. Your choices have a ripple effect on the people around you. Be the person you want to be. Pursue the change you want to see.
- Pray and then pray some more. Pray for God's wisdom, discernment, direction, and next steps for you. Ask someone to pray with and/or for you.

- Spend time with God in His Word—this is another game changer! The SOAP Method I share with you at the end of each chapter is practical, easy, and something you can put in your devotional toolbox and use any time as a way of connecting with God. When you're hurting or not doing well, reading the Bible may be the last thing you want to do. Please consider making it the first thing you do. When I'm struggling, this is the first place I check to see how I'm doing with reading my Bible. God's Word is alive and active, and it's the #1 place we need to go to hear from God to know what He is calling us to do.

- Ask God for wisdom, people, and resources to help you identify and process your past and present hurts. Learn about healthy relationships and how to resolve your hurts to experience healing and wholeness. Don't do this alone. I've personally benefited from one-on-one counseling and group counseling—I needed both. Often you will find Bible-believing churches that offer group programs. As I've mentioned, we have an amazing program at our church called Breakthrough, which is a biblically-based 12-week healing journey.

- Find books to read, take a course, or do a Bible Study. (*Living Beyond Yourself* and *Breaking Free*, both by Beth Moore, are studies I've found helpful in recent years.)

- Be willing to begin the forgiveness process. *Learn what forgiveness is and what it isn't.* I believe in asking others for forgiveness. I also believe in forgiving others, not because I feel like it or they deserve it but for the freedom I receive giving everything to God and giving up the right to seek retribution for what they have done. I believe forgiveness is a process and something I can safely have a conversation with God about, remembering that sometimes it's not safe and does not always mean speaking with the other person or seeking reconciliation with them.

- Pray with others. The Bible says, "Therefore confess your sins to each other and pray for each other so that you may be healed. The prayer of a righteous person is powerful and effective" (James 5:16 NIV).

Pray for people to come along beside you and pray for, encourage, and care for you. Keep short accounts with God. Prayer is something I will share more about in Chapter 11 and how it is your secret weapon when it comes to your Freedom.

- Ask Jesus to heal your broken heart and free you to love and receive love.

5. FREE—What does it look like? What do you do now?

It takes one generation to break the cycle of hurt, turn their hearts toward God, and be free to live out their God-given destiny. These brave Freedom Fighters and Truth Tellers pass on a legacy of faith and God's love to their children and the next generation. It takes only one. Be the one to stand and fight.

The reason we want to be free from the hurts inside is so that we can reach the potential God has for us. God wants us to close the gap and seek healing so that we can have a meaningful relationship with Him and do the work that He purposed for us to do.

"God saved you by his grace when you believed. And you can't take credit for this; it is a gift from God. Salvation is not a reward for the good things we have done, so none of us can boast about it. For **we are God's masterpiece**. He has created us anew in Christ Jesus, **so we can do the good things he planned for us long ago**." (Ephesians 2:8–10 NLT)

So what now? What's next? Personally, I think Jesus' mission is our mission. He came to this earth to set the captives, like me, free. Here's what the Bible says about Jesus' purpose for coming here—

"The Spirit of the Lord is on me, because he has anointed me to proclaim good news to the poor. He has sent me to proclaim freedom for the prisoners and recovery of sight for the blind, to set the oppressed free, to proclaim the year of the Lord's favor." (Luke 4:18–19 NIV)

"Christ has set us free to live a free life. So take your stand! Never again let anyone put a harness of slavery on you." (Galatians 5:1 The Message)

You'll hear me say often that free people can help free people. I appreciate how Eugene Peterson summarized Galatians 5:13–15 in The Message—

"It is absolutely clear that God has called you to a free life. Just make sure that you don't use this freedom as an excuse to do whatever you want to do and destroy your freedom. Rather, use your freedom to serve one another in love; that's how freedom grows. For everything we know about God's Word is summed up in a single sentence: Love others as you love yourself. That's an act of true freedom. If you bite and ravage each other, watch out—in no time at all you will be anni-hilating each other, and where will your precious freedom be then?"

This is going to get heavy really quick. I'm picturing someone with a broken heart. Heart-sinking news—loss of hope—that feeling when you've been crushed and you feel like you can't breathe anymore. The pit of your stomach falling. Grief. Loss. A "Will I ever survive this?" kind of feeling.

That hole in your heart. The void. Maybe you look to fill it, or maybe you don't. Who will fill it? What will fill it? You look to numb the pain, please people, keep busy, and find distractions or ways you can escape. You try to control the situation. You can't. Your coping mechanisms fail you.

Trust me, I'm preaching to the choir. I've done it all. I've felt it all—up until I arrived at the place where "I know that I know" that nothing BUT Jesus can fill the void or the holes in my life and my heart. Jesus came to pick up all the pieces and heal my broken heart. To set me free from the prison or cage around my heart. To free me to love and receive love. To offer me a freedom I did not know I did not have.

In finding a voice for my pain and giving my hurts and wounds to God, He exchanged them for healed wounds that are there but don't hurt any more.

Free people can free people.

Be free, and be the one who fights for and sets others free.

Your Sacred Time, Space, and Calling

15-Minute Freedom Exercise

I can't tell you how much I appreciate the Freedom Fighters and Truth Tellers God has brought into my life. This freedom exercise—a self-evaluation of sorts—I'm passing along is something a mentor of mine shared with me.

Take a blank sheet of paper or journal page, and draw a line down the middle of the page. On the right side of the page, at the top, put a positive "+" sign. On the left side, at the top of the page, put a negative "-" sign.

Take some time to reflect and read this verse out loud as a way to start—

"Search me, God, and know my heart; test me and know my anxious thoughts. See if there is any offensive way in me, and lead me in the way everlasting." (Psalm 139:23–24 NIV)

Start with the positives first. Take some time to pray. Ask God to prepare your heart to hear what He has to say to you. Ask Him to share with you the positive traits He sees in you. Take some time. Listen. Write down the thoughts that come to mind. Once you have completed writing the positives, ask God about the negatives. Write them down on the other side of the cross.

Take some time to look at the negative list. Confess the list to God—my prayer is often "Lord Jesus, I am sorry and confess each of these negative attributes (say them one by one) and ask you for forgiveness in how they have played out in my life. Please help me to be a person of integrity and grow in character to become more like you." It's powerful when you pray your prayers out loud. Then ask God to fill the places where these negatives characteristics took up residency in your life and replace the negative attributes with all that He intends for you. Pray for the Holy Spirit to fill you with the Fruit of the Spirit—"But the fruit of the Spirit is love, joy, peace, forbearance, kindness, goodness, faithfulness, gentleness and self-control. Against such things there is no law." (Galatians 5:22–23 NIV)

Now it's time to pray about the positives. My favorite part. My prayer is often "Lord, I give back to you these positive characteristics you see in me. Please cleanse and purify them and return them back to me for your purposes to be accomplished in my life. May what I say and do be for your glory and honor. In Jesus' name, Amen."

This evaluation is something that is good to do on a periodic basis, and definitely if you are struggling, it is a good next step. On the day that I'm writing this to you, my positives list was long. *So lovely*, I thought. But my negatives list was equally long. *Sigh!* Yes, reality was not the encouragement I was hoping for on this challenging day. But God is good, and I love how He surprises me. After my prayer, I sensed God directing me to some verses in the Bible, especially one verse, a promise that had been given to my family that I had forgotten about, and two other scripture passages that I read and felt encouraged by as I received the truth in love that God had for me that day. As a dear friend often reminds me, "God is good ALL the time."

SPECIAL TIME WITH GOD
Set aside 15 minutes. Read **PSALM 32** in the Old Testament. You may consider reading the passage a second time out loud. What verse sticks out or connects with you? Apply the SOAP Method.

S – Scripture – Write out the verse you chose. Write it in this space below or in your journal.

_____

_____

_____

O – Observation – What are one or two facts that you observe from the verse you chose?

_____

_____

_____

A – Application – How can you personally apply this verse to your life?

_____

_____

_____

P – Prayer – Write out a prayer to God related to your reading today. There is no right or wrong way to do this. Prayer is having a conversation with God. Think of this as a conversation starter between you and God.

_____

_____

_____

PRAYER AND ENCOURAGEMENT
Be sure to **STOP**, **pray**, and **listen**.

I have seen real life change and the value of turning down the noise and listening for God's wisdom, encouragement, and direction for my life. It may be a word. It may be a Scripture passage. It may be encouragement tailor made just for you. It may be a sense that you are to reach out to a community for help, prayer, and support. It may be that you've experienced some God-given freedom, and it's time for you to share your message of hope and healing to change your world around you.

Pray! Be sure to stop and pray—ask for God's help and direction at every corner. The still, small voice whispering encouragement to you along the way—be confident it's God. Listen to that voice!

God never gives up on you; He never leaves you. He never lets go of you. When you are about ready to give up, remember, He hasn't!

Keep taking the next step. Whether you are in the valley, halfway up the mountain, or almost there, keep going. Just keep going.

8

THE BEST VERSION

"He made you—on purpose. You are the only you—ever. Becoming ourselves means we are actively cooperating with God's intention for our lives, not fighting him or ourselves. He looks at us with pleasure and with mercy, and he wants us to look at ourselves with pleasure and mercy too!"

STASI ELDREDGE, *BECOMING MYSELF: EMBRACING GOD'S DREAM OF YOU*

IT SEEMED LIKE when I picked our daughter up at the bus stop in the first grade, she was a different child than when I said goodbye in the morning. She'd run towards me upset, throwing her backpack on the ground and storming off in the direction of our home.

I thought to myself, *Is she tired? Is she hungry?* To be honest, I found it challenging to know how to help and not get agitated myself in the process. After a day of missing her, I selfishly hoped for a hug and smile and an "I'm so glad to see you too, Mommy!"

One day, after recognizing a definite pattern developing, I decided to dig a little deeper.

"I've noticed you are really upset with me, and I want to be able to help you. I'm wondering, can you share with me how you are feeling when you are getting off the school bus?"

She looked at me, and I looked at her.

She then blurted out, "Mommy, I've used up all my niceness at school, and I don't have anything left!"

Wow! I tried not to smile at the amazing insight our six-year-old girl had just revealed to me. The fact that she could identify what had been happening for her and articulate it in this manner showed a tremendous amount of self-awareness on her part.

My initial response was to hug her, and with a sense of relief, I then went on to say, "Thank you for sharing—I hear what you are saying, Sunshine. This will help me know how to help you."

Inside, part of me understood. Part of me could relate, even as an adult. Part of me felt not equipped to respond. Then I thought about what helped me personally when I felt this way. I had an idea of how I could help my daughter. We started a new routine that day. I made up a snack plate and helped her get settled in a quiet area where she played with her toys and watched a short TV show. When she finished, she then came to find me, happy and all smiles, ready to share about her day. This new routine helped our daughter greatly. It allowed her to recharge from her full day at school and thrive, as opposed to struggle, when she arrived home. A quiet time after school is something she continues to enjoy years later—and she has her own special area at the end of our upstairs hallway.

To help her further, I looked for ways to equip myself to respond not only to my children's physical needs but their emotional needs as well. I heard about a parenting workshop at our local Christian counseling center. The course was in a group setting for a series of ten weeks. The program is called CPR—Child Parent Relationship.[1]

From what I understand, when therapists meet with children, they tend to use play therapy as opposed to talk therapy. The idea is that playing is children's language, and toys are their words. In the course, we as parents learned how to have special playtime sessions with our kids, which included child-directed play, identifying how our kids are feeling, and setting boundaries for our child. This life-changing course has provided me with tremendous insight and perspective on my children's emotional needs. And my own for that matter.

In making the decision to Break the Cycle of Hurt, this course helped me learn more about healthy and secure relationships and how to provide a healthy environment for our kids. I've had special playtime sessions with both our children, and they love it. It has brought our relationships to a deeper and closer level. Growth choices like this can be humbling and challenging yet also an amazing opportunity to connect, invest, and build into a relationship with your child.

I've learned how to respond to my kids in a way that they know that I hear, understand, and care for them, even when I don't agree with what they are doing. In responding to my children, I don't always get this right. What I do know is that God gets this right. He cares, understands, and hears us—all the time. This parenting course got me thinking about how we as humans were created to spend time and connect with our Creator—to have our own "Special Time with God." God's presence is a space and place where I believe He comforts, encourages, strengthens, directs, heals, helps, and fills our love and energy tanks—so that we can thrive, grow, and do what He calls us to do. It's a gift and a benefit as a child of God that I don't want to miss out on.

Like I desire with my kids, I think God wants to have close a relationship with us—His kids—and spend time with us one on one. He knows everything that is going on in our lives. The Bible says that God knows what we are going to say even before we say it.[2] And He still wants to spend time with us because He cares about and enjoys our company.

Someone I appreciate and consider to be a mentor is Dr. Ron Gannett, who has an incredible heart to equip leaders.[3] His goal is to help people help people. He shared the SOAP Bible Study Method at a week-long conference I attended last summer. Each day we applied the SOAP Method to a Bible reading on our own, and some of us shared with the group at the opening of each teaching session. I felt like I had been given a real gift, and I'm thankful for the opportunity to pass along this devotional tool to you. The SOAP Method came at a time when I was tired and overwhelmed, and it became a way that God encouraged and filled me up again. I like this study method because it's practical and easy and it provides an intentional space to meet with God. I think if we are honest, we all desire to have a good relationship or a deeper relationship with God.

With the SOAP Method, after you write out your prayer, consider taking some time to journal and take your conversation with God to a deeper level—an honest, "what's really going on" conversation with God. I think it's crucial to share with God when we are hurt or we are experiencing pain; it also applies when we are celebrating something and feeling joy. Be intentional about finding a voice to express what's going on inside. Like with our daughter, who had the self-awareness that she was "on empty" after a long day at school, God wants to hear from us daily on how we are doing. I encourage you to find a voice for your pain and your joy. Share your feelings with God—both positive and negative.

Often I think when we are feeling negative emotions and feelings we don't always want to talk about it. With the emotional hurt I experienced in the last year, I felt overwhelmed, angry, bitter, and fearful. I think it is sometimes easier to go to God when we are thankful or to pray for others or ask Him for surface needs. It's not easy to go beneath the surface and look to see what is going on behind the negative feelings we are experiencing.

What I find helpful is letting God know how I am feeling and asking Him to speak truth and encouragement into my situation. I like to journal when I do this; for instance, you can do this after your SOAP prayer time. Share with God one feeling at a time. In my circumstance I described, first I asked about being overwhelmed, then angry, etc. Praying something like,

"Lord, these feelings of being overwhelmed…what do you want to say to me through what I'm feeling?"

"Please speak to me, Lord. Help me hear your voice clearly."

"What encouragement do you want to say to me?"

"What lies am I believing about this situation?"

"What healing truth do you have for me?"

When negative feelings come to the surface, this alerts me to take some time to journal and spend time with God. When I felt hurt this past year, I sensed God saying, *"This is something you are not meant to carry."* The heavy feelings pushed and weighed down on me, but it was not my burden to carry. Now when I feel overwhelmed, I am quicker to ask, "Lord, what am I carrying that I'm not meant to carry?" This is a regular practice I do with God.

Personally, I've found that when negative feelings are coming to the surface, it's best to ask God about them. This is not something you do alone. I know personally I've needed to reach out to community on many occasions—at times by way of a trusted friend who talked and prayed with me, a coach, a mentor, or one of our pastors, or I've met with a counselor to further process how I'm feeling. The point is, don't ignore your feelings—they are there in front of you or coming to the surface for a reason. Talk with God, and ask Him to speak encouragement, truth, and wisdom into how you are feeling. Ask Him WHAT'S NEXT on your journey to freedom, healing, and wholeness.

Is it just me? Do you connect with anything that I'm sharing? Did you know you could talk with God and ask Him to speak into your life this way?

When I feel burdened or tired or when I'm struggling, there are three areas of my life that I like to check. I find when I'm not connected to them, this is when I can get myself into some trouble. When I am connected, I feel recharged and more equipped to face life's challenges and thrive as opposed to just survive—kind of like building up my "niceness reserve" and having my "love tank filled" when I'm running on empty.

So what are the three areas? I believe we are the best version of ourselves when we are connected to our Creator, Core, and Community. What does this mean? This is a topic that I am extremely passionate about and something I've been journeying through and thinking about more intentionally over the past number of years. I'm thankful for the coaches and mentors in my life who have helped me gain perspective on this topic even further.

Here's a diagram I've put together for you to help illustrate:

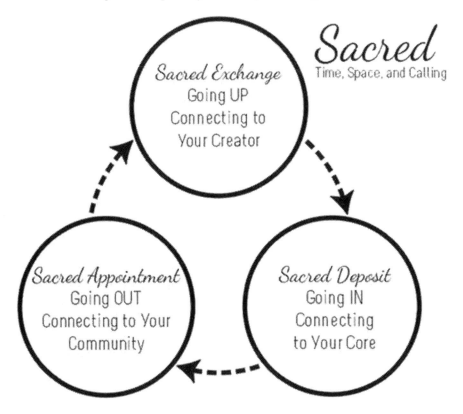

1. Sacred Exchange—Going UP—Connecting to Your Creator

    Let me start by saying who I mean by Creator. Personally, I am referring to the God of the Bible and the Creator of Heaven and Earth. Did you know that this God I'm talking about loves you and created you to know Him, not from a distance but personally? The Bible tells us that God created you:

    > "You made all the delicate, inner parts of my body and knit me together in my mother's womb. Thank you for making me so wonderfully complex! Your workmanship is marvelous—how well I know it." (Psalm 139:13–14 NLT)

To expand further, my personal connection to God is through a personal relationship with Jesus Christ. This connection is a personal relationship with a loving God who deeply cares for the world.

"For this is how God loved the world: He gave his one and only Son, so that everyone who believes in him will not perish but have eternal life. God sent his Son into the world not to judge the world, but to save the world through him." (John 3:16–17 NLT)

Do you have a personal relationship with God? Are you at peace with Him?

If you have a relationship with Jesus, it's the best decision you have ever made, in my opinion. If you don't know if you do or you are not sure, I hope it's something you will question and consider. I think if you have a desire to be all you've been created to be, it starts with having this personal relationship and receiving God's free gift of salvation. And know that when you do this, it's the beginning of a beautiful, intimate, and growing friendship with a personal and loving Savior.

If you know Jesus and you find you're struggling, can I share a good self-check I use? I simply ask myself some questions: "How is my devotional life?" More specifically, how am I making my quiet time with God and reading and studying the Bible a priority in my life?

This is why I like the SOAP Method that I'm sharing with you at the end of each chapter. "Your Special Time with God" is an amazing way to grow in your relationship with Jesus. This is time for just you and God. When we discover the truth God has for us in His Word, we have the opportunity to carry on a conversation with Him throughout the day about what He has brought to light. What I think happens in these times is a beautiful exchange—where when I'm GOING UP to spend time with God. He orchestrates this Sacred Exchange.

My uncertainty for His clarity.

My unworthiness for His forgiveness.

My discouragement for His hope and encouragement.

My lack of feeling equipped for His wisdom and empowering.

My false beliefs for His healing truth.

My hurts for His healing and care for my heart.

My sadness for His joy.

My tiredness for His rest.

What about you? Where would you like to ask God to orchestrate a Sacred Exchange in your life? You could say—

God, please exchange my _____ for your_____.

I am the best version of me when I'm connected to my Creator—my Lord God and Savior. I've found that when I do this, it encourages me and fosters peace and contentment in my heart, a desire for a deeper relationship with God (and other people), growing understanding of God's Word, knowing God more intimately, learning more about myself, finding a voice for my pain and my story, being thankful and praising God, experiencing healing and restoration, and feeling rested and recharged to serve others. What an amazing incentive to look up to God!

2. Sacred Deposits—Going IN—Connecting to Your Core

Your Core? Is this a workout? It is of sorts. I like to think of your Core as closely linked to your calling in life. I think every human being on this earth has a desire to be loved and accepted and to make a difference in this world.

My passion and calling and the song of my heart is "Connecting People to a Love That Is Calling Their Name." I'm passionate about helping people connect to their Creator and also to their own purpose and passions—specifically, what they love in life and are gifted and created to do. This is a high-level explanation. I go into this on a deeper level in my coaching programs. To summarize, I think there are three themes of questions every person wonders about and has a desire to find answers for:

- Who am I? More specifically, what is my identity?
- Why am I here? What's my purpose, and why am I on this earth?
- What's next for me? How can I put my purpose into action?

I believe God wants us to have clarity and confidence in knowing our identity and purpose and WHO He says we are. This is foundational to knowing more about our God-given calling and WHY we are here on this earth.

This type of clarity requires time and investment in yourself—GOING IN and making regular deposits—or Sacred Deposits—towards your personal, physical, emotional, and spiritual well-being. Spending time and resources by investing in your growth and development is essential to connecting to your Core and the best version of you. What are the Sacred Deposits you plan on making in your life to fully connect with WHO and WHY you were created to be?

Here are some questions my coach shared with me that I've personally found helpful in connecting to my Core.[4] At first glance, I thought, *These questions will be easy to answer—I've done some of this work before.* It turned out to be one of those easier said than done tasks although well worth the clarity and strength I received as a result of the hard work. A good friend of ours, Brett Ullman, is a gifted speaker and Truth Teller who travels North America conversing with teens, young adults, leaders, and parents on challenging topics not often discussed inside or outside the church.[5] He shares in his talks that our worldview shapes our values and our values shape our actions. Wow! This drives home the need to articulate our own beliefs and values because they highly influence the direction of our lives. I hope you will take some time to journal about these questions and find this self-discovery process encouraging to you. We'll expand more on this in the "WHY Are You Here?" chapter.

- Worldview—What do I believe?
- Identity—Who am I?
- Principles—What do I value?
- Passion—Who and what do I love?
- Purpose—Why do I live and work?
- Process—How do I do it?

3. Sacred Appointments—Going OUT—Connecting to Your Community

Personally, I am a huge advocate of finding a faith community where you can connect, heal, and grow. I've seen this in my own life, where I have thrived in a community and where I have not grown in others. If you are a follower of Jesus, there is no substitute for the local church. This is not always easy. People have been hurt in faith communities. I've been hurt in my church. Maybe you've been hurt or have given up on the church. Or maybe you think the church is irrelevant, and you are not interested in going at all.

I'm not saying our church is the best church out there. Right now, it is the best church for me and my family. If you find you are somewhere for a while and you want to leave for some reason, ask yourself—is this my stuff or the church's stuff? If it's your issue, I challenge you to stop and reconsider leaving. I say this in the most loving way. I challenge you to seek what change you need for yourself. If you are not sure, it's okay. Ask God, and He will reveal it to you. If you are in a church that can help you, specifically one that takes or encourages a holistic approach (which supports meeting the physical, spiritual, and emotional needs of its members), I would encourage you to stay and then see what you would like to do after you have experienced the healing and restoration God has for you. Maybe this is the reason God brought you to this particular church. God brought our family to the steps of our current church, and it then became *our choice* to connect with others, to be open to God's healing, and to pursue spiritual growth and maturity.

When I mentor and coach groups of people, again and again they share the value of being in community and learning and growing in fellowship together. We are not meant to journey alone. God in His nature is all about community—as we think about God the Father, God the Son, and the God Holy Spirit. Our community is very much linked to our purpose and our callings as we go out into our community and serve others the way God has gifted us.

Look for a local church where you are encouraged, where you can ask hard questions, where you can safely heal from hurts, and where you can connect in a healthy way with others beyond the surface to learn, make mistakes, thrive, and grow. It needs to be the RIGHT community for you—and really, don't give up until you find it. You will know when you do. The local church is not perfect, and it's been said the church can in ways resemble one big, dysfunctional family. You want a church that aims to move from being dysfunctional to functional and towards their full potential. You want a church where their core values are aligned with God's Word and His plans and purposes. You want a church that is clear on what they believe and where they stand. You want a church where you feel valued, seen, and heard.

I've personally experienced freedom and healing that I don't think would have happened had we not moved to the church we now attend. We've made friends and have had many people come alongside our family to pray with us and for us. Some of these friends are people who have prayed for you as I am writing this book. We are blessed to be a part of an encouraging and life-giving small group. These have become close friendships where we serve each other, where we can ask challenging questions about our faith, where we look to have more meaningful discussions, and where we journey through the highs and lows of life together. I'm thankful for the pastors, coaches, and mentors God has brought into my life who have poured into me directly or indirectly. We are incredibly thankful for our church and the many opportunities to be ministered to and pursue the freedom, wholeness, and healing God has had for us. We need community and people to be the hands and feet of Jesus to us and us to them. Remember, churches and faith communities are not perfect. But neither are we.

Where are you with connecting with your Creator, Core, and Community? I'm hoping your soul has been encouraged and that you are inspired to take these connections to a new level. I'm praying for you and cheering you on. I believe in you.

I have to share this with you. I'm sitting here struggling to finish this chapter for some reason, and a friend just called me on Skype. She saw me logged in and called to say hi and to do what she does best—to bless and encourage me. She asked about my book and how the writing has been going. I shared I'd been fighting doubt, fear of failure, and perfectionism, and she simply said, "Anything you write will be good. I love reading your emails, so I can only imagine how encouraging your book will be to me. I can't wait to read it."

Wow, what a beautiful Sacred Appointment! I needed to hear this—it gave me the boost I needed to keep pushing through this crazy resistance. My friend is a natural encourager. Her words of blessing go straight to my heart. We all need friends like this in our lives.

But wait, there's this nagging feeling coming to the surface. This "I'm not connected" feeling. How is this possible? I'm writing a chapter about "connecting." This picture is coming to mind. I'm seeing someone on the outside looking in and not part of the crowd. Have you ever had the "I don't fit in" feeling? I know that feeling. I know it well. I've fought against that feeling. The fact is I do belong. I am accepted, significant, and loved. So are you! Shame tells us a different story. Shame whispers in our ear and tells us we are not worthy of connection with God and others.

Being vulnerable and sharing our freedom story brings shame out into the light, and it loses its power. We think we need to have it all together before we can connect to God, others, and even our calling. We wear a mask and think if people really knew me, they would not accept me.

This is not God's plan. He accepts and meets you just where you are. God made only one YOU—on purpose for His purposes. You are accepted and worthy of connection with your Creator, your Core, and your Community.

The Bible says, "So now there is no condemnation for those who belong to Christ Jesus." (Romans 8:1 NLT)

Freedom is found here—being the best version of you is BEING YOU!

YOUR SACRED TIME, SPACE, AND CALLING

15-MINUTE FREEDOM EXERCISE

We are the **best version** of ourselves when we are connected to our **Creator, Core**, and **Community**.

What comes to mind when you read this?

_____

_____

_____

If this interests you, what are ways you can connect on a deeper level to your Creator, Core, and Community?

_____

_____

_____

I encourage you to create some margin in your life and invest in yourself and this tremendously important calling on your life. I've created a space for you in the "Prayer and Encouragement" section to carry on this conversation. I'll continue to share more on these topics in the chapters to come.

SPECIAL TIME WITH GOD

Set aside 15 minutes. Read **PSALM 63** in the Old Testament. You may consider reading it a second time out loud. What verse sticks out or connects with you? Apply the SOAP Method.

S – Scripture – Write out the verse you chose. Write it in this space below or in your journal.

_____

_____

_____

O – Observation – What are one or two facts that you observe from the verse you chose?

_____

_____

_____

A – Application – How can you personally apply this verse to your life?

_____

_____

_____

P – Prayer – Write out a prayer to God related to your reading today. There is no right or wrong way to do this. Prayer is having a conversation with God. Think of this as a conversation starter between you and God.

_____

_____

_____

PRAYER AND ENCOURAGEMENT

How are you connecting to your Creator, Core, and Community?

Pray! Ask God to help you in these three areas. Ask Him to give you 1) a fresh perspective on how to connect on a deeper level and close any gaps in your growing relationship with Him, 2) clarity on WHO you are, WHY you are here, your purpose on this earth, and WHAT'S NEXT for you (two questions I find helpful to ask—what is God telling me and what is He asking me to do?), and 3) insight into how you can connect further to the community and the world around you. Ask God for the next steps in living out your calling in a way that He intends. Who are the people you are to fellowship with and serve? Are you connected to a local church? How do you share your faith with others? What are ways you can connect with others? Who are you encouraging, and who is encouraging you?

Next take some time to listen to what God is saying to you. This is important. Prayer is a two-way conversation between you and God. Ask God your questions one at a time, and listen to what He has to say to you. His words are convicting, truthful, encouraging, helpful, loving, and kind. This is how you know it is God. Be confident that He hears you and will respond to you. What comes to mind? Try journaling your thoughts. Know that God cares for you, loves you, and wants to bless you.

_____

_____

9

CLOSING THE GAPS

"We cannot become what we need to be by remaining what we are."

MAX DE PREE

I CURIOUSLY FOLLOW MISSIONARIES. I've been doing it for a while now. It's not something I've been conscious about until I started connecting the dots recently. It turns out I have quite a few friends who are missionaries—well, maybe not in the traditional sense, but some are. I just searched online the word mission: "an important assignment carried out for political, religious, or commercial purposes, typically involving travel."[21]

An important assignment. Hmm. That sounds appealing to me. How about you? Wouldn't we all like to be on an important assignment? Maybe you are on one already. Maybe you would like to be on one. We often think of missionaries as those who travel to faraway countries or, in the case of some of my friends, people who live in towns like you and me and carry out their day with purpose and on a mission.

Deep inside, we all want to know that we are accepted and valued and that we are making a significant contribution to our world. I'm incredibly thankful that I believe in and serve a God who is an issuer of important assignments in the church. Our dream and vision for our life is really our mission. It's a dream I believe God places in each and every heart on this planet, and it's linked to His unique plans and purposes. "God has now revealed to us his mysterious plan regarding Christ, a plan to fulfill his own good pleasure. And this is the plan: At the right time he will bring everything together under the authority of Christ—everything in heaven and on earth. Furthermore, because we are united with Christ, we have received an inheritance from God, for he chose us in advance, and he makes everything work out according to his plan" (Ephesians 1:9–11 NLT).

Do you believe you are on this earth for a significant purpose? Maybe you've thought about it but you've not seen it happen, or there's been a time when you felt you were on the right road but you're currently experiencing a detour. Maybe you have not taken time to think about it. Maybe you have clarity on your purpose and calling, but there are some areas of your life that are not cooperating.

I've been there—and I'm still there in some cases. We all need to have a BIG DREAM. Whether you are a person of faith or not, you need to dream and have a vision for your life. This is a passion of mine—helping others see potential in themselves that they may not see. I actually didn't know I had this dream in my heart, and it's been through the process of closing the gaps in my life that I discovered it.

You may be wondering what I am referring to when I say "Closing the Gaps." This is a topic I could share about in great length—maybe because I've had so many gaps to close in my life. In the pages to follow, I've outlined five questions, which I'll elaborate on, and we will see how far we get. Remember, these are areas I've worked through personally in my life—I'm preaching to myself when I share this with you.

1. What are some gaps?

- Closing the gap from having no margin to having margin—setting aside time to invest and take time for your life (and those you care about) to work on the areas where you would like to see change and experience freedom
- Closing the gap from where you are now to where you want to be
- Closing the gap between you and God. Do you have peace with God? Do you have a personal relationship with Jesus Christ? If so, what, if anything, is standing in the way of a deeper, growing relationship?
- Closing the gap from feeling uncertain and fearful to feeling confident and faith filled.
- Closing the gap from having a perspective of self-help to seeking God's help and direction
- Closing the gap from bondage and sin (personal, generational, and blind spots) to becoming aware, turning away from sin, and being set free
- Closing the gap from being hurt inside to being healed and free to be who you were created to be
- Closing the gap between your purpose and the significant calling on your life—breaking free from the caged places and the distraction traps that keep you bound
- Closing the gap from what you say you believe and how you live
- Closing the gap from feeling unprepared to feeling equipped to live out your important calling in life
- Closing the gap from what you say you value and your actions.
- Closing the gap from talking about what you are doing and doing it.
- Closing the gap from not being connected in a local church to being connected and thriving and growing in your faith community
- Closing the gap from being a people pleaser to a God pleaser who loves people and is a "truth in love" teller
- Closing the gap from who you are and who you want to be

- Closing the gap in the important relationships in your life from a superficial connection to being genuinely connected in love
- Closing the gap from a prideful heart to a humble heart
- Closing the gap from being a victim to a victor—from feeling unable to being empowered
- Closing the gap from being undeveloped to experiencing spiritual growth and maturity in your faith
- Closing the gap from having no voice to having a voice to share your story
- Closing the gap from an overwhelmed heart to a free and restored heart
- Closing the gap from having no dream and vision for your life to living out your purpose and BIG DREAM
- Closing the gap from a legacy you inherited to an eternal legacy you want to pass on

2. What's standing in the way?

I know this about myself. You may know it about yourself too. The biggest obstacle in my life is actually ME! Add this to the resistance and additional obstacles that come my way and I've found myself in a perfect storm of defeat, discouragement, and distraction.

An example is writing this book. I can't tell you how many roadblocks, detours, and flat tires have surfaced. Just in the last month alone I've had computer issues, and my website hosting company took down my website because it had been hacked. Thankfully, I have backups of my work, and although it took quite some time to resolve, my website is up and running again. These were big distractions, and they took time to deal with, which limited the amount of time for writing and editing. It was hard to get back into it and gain momentum again. These types of transitions can be challenging, but it's often the "good things" that can distract me even further. I've found the best strategy is to pray, ask others to pray, push through the resistance, and get back to this "great thing" of finishing my book. The fact that you are reading this means that thankfully, with God's help, I've been successful.

3. What do I need in order to do this?
Here's what comes to mind, in no particular order—

- Investment of your time and resources
- Teachable spirit
- Coachable
- Accountability
- Humility
- Prayer
- More prayer
- A heart willing and open to change
- Connection to God and His wisdom and direction
- God's help and the help of others—don't do it alone
- Connection to your community—you are not alone
- Confidence in WHO you are (your identity)
- Clarity on WHY you are here (your purpose)
- Consistent time in God's Word
- Freedom Fighters and Truth Tellers in your life

4. What do I do in the waiting?
Awareness unlocks the door to truth, hope, healing, freedom, and whole-ness in your life. Hope is incredibly important to hang on to, and al-though it's not a strategy in itself, you need it to breathe life into your plan and put wind back into your sails.

There are many steps we can take in the process of closing our gaps. As I mentioned, one of my first responses is to pray—pray, pray, and pray some more. I'll share more on this in Chapter 11.

Stay focused on your personal growth and healing. I find I can get distracted with opportunities to help and serve others. Recently I needed to say "no" to an amazing opportunity so that I could fully receive the wisdom and experience the healing in my life that I needed *before* I could go on to help others. It may seem like there's never a good time to focus on your own healing. Stick with it. Set aside time. Step back from responsibilities if you need to. Have the conversations you've been putting off or avoiding. Spend time with God. Journal your thoughts and feelings. Make the appointment with a counselor, if needed. Be willing to look beneath the surface. Stop trying to fix and figure things out. Do the hard work that you need to do to close the gaps you so desire.

Take time to get to know yourself. Ask yourself the hard questions, and be intentional about answering them. If you need some help in this area, ask a coach or mentor to help you identify some questions to ask. In this process of becoming, your character is important. Your choices and motives matter. They shape who you are. Look at where, what, and with whom you are spending your time. Is this aligned with the gaps you want to close in your life?

5. How do I know how I'm doing?
   "A goal is not about what you accomplish. It's about what you become."[2]
   Michael Hyatt

   This quote says it exceptionally well. It's a more elegant way of saying, "I'm a work in progress." My coach has instilled this "process of becoming" concept in me, and I share it with my coaching clients. If you are a follower of Jesus, it's even more relevant as you grow in His likeness and character.

   This process of becoming who you were created to be and, really, undoing who you were not created to be, will transform your life. Growth in awareness empowers you and reminds you of the possibilities. Having people come alongside you—to mentor, coach, truth tell, invest in you, and notice your growth—will encourage and motivate you to move forward. Be open! And keep moving!

This week one of my mentors sat with me and gave it to me straight. She didn't hold back. We have an agreement, and she is committed to keeping me accountable in one particular area of my life—specifically my time with God "just for me" and with no other agenda.

First, let me say this sounds easy, yet I find it to be a challenging task. It's something I think we can have the best of intentions concerning, but life gets busy or is going well, and it gets overlooked. And besides, work, ministry, and serving others is spending time with God, right?

Personally, I like to help people and share what I'm learning. One of the aspects I enjoyed about being a financial associate was offering people advice on how to invest their money and plan for their future. My heart has always been to encourage people, and it comes naturally when I'm learning something new to think about how I can share it with others.

So back to my time with God. I've learned this lesson sometimes the hard way—that I need to position myself to receive the wisdom God has for me and apply it to my life first. It's that simple.

Transformation happens when I discover and walk in the truth of God's Word for myself and then help others out of the overflow of my experience and understanding. My life and heart need to be impacted first, and then I can extend the learning to others simply because I can't teach what I have not learned myself.

My time with God is a source of encouragement. This time fills me with what I need to go out and encourage and care for my family, friends, and the people that cross my path each day. Does this make sense or resonate with you? Is it just me who finds this difficult to live out?

As someone who loves to write and create resources, I need to resist the temptation to say, "Oh, I can use this for here and for there and for that person who I am teaching or I care about." It needs to be for THIS person—ME first. My ongoing prayer needs to be "God, make the changes in me."

And yet it seems that when life gets busy—like this week, when my husband is away on a business trip, we're looking for a contractor for some home repairs, and I'm caring for our kids, working, editing my book, and planning for school ending and summer to begin. Do you find your schedule can be busy or is getting busier? I don't know about you, but it's these times when I find that my time to be still and quiet can get cut short, or I may even skip it that day. It is okay if this happens. I often say to the people I mentor and coach to "be kind to yourself." I just know if I go too long without spending time in God's Word, I can get myself in a lot of trouble—I start to feel drained before I finally clue in to the absence and benefit of being in God's presence. The SOAP Bible Study Method is a practical and easy way to discover God's Word for yourself and not just survive but thrive in your busy world. I find SOAP is a real conversation starter, and when I'm using it, I get excited and can't wait to chat with and see what knowledge and wisdom God has for me that day.

As I've shared previously, and what I continue to learn, is that I am the best version of myself when I make time to spend with my Creator. With this ongoing connection, I am more equipped to do what God is telling me and asking me to do. "So here's what I want you to do, God helping you: Take your everyday, ordinary life—your sleeping, eating, going-to-work, and walking-around life—and place it before God as an offering. Embracing what God does for you is the best thing you can do for him. Don't become so well-adjusted to your culture that you fit into it without even thinking. Instead, fix your attention on God. You'll be changed from the inside out. Readily recognize what he wants from you, and quickly respond to it. Unlike the culture around you, always dragging you down to its level of immaturity, God brings the best out of you, develops well-formed maturity in you" Romans 12:1–2 (The Message).

Is this statement true or false? It is good to include God in your plans.

What do you think?

When I first heard it, I thought, *Yes! I'm in. That's exactly what I do!*

The statement is in fact a FALSE STATEMENT.

The truth is God does not want to be involved in your plans; He wants you to be included in HIS plan. And HIS plan is to disciple the nations.

Well, this rocked my world completely. Five years ago this new awareness helped me close a major gap in my life. In the summertime, our family tradition is to go for a vacation to a family camp or retreat center. This is a treasured time when we are deeply encouraged, have our energy and love tanks filled, have fun, and grow spiritually. I've had the privilege of hearing Dr. George Murray speak for a full week on two occasions.[3] He is from Columbia International University and one of my favorite summer conference speakers. He's the person who posed this question, and through it, God upset this apple cart of mine.

There's something called the Great Commission. You may or may not have heard of it. Basically, it represents Jesus' last words to His disciples before He went back to heaven, where now He sits alive and to the right hand of God the Father. His disciples, if you don't know about them, are Jesus' original followers, whom He mentored and trained to share the freedom of the gospel story with the world. Here's what He said:

> "Then Jesus came to them and said, 'All authority in heaven and on earth has been given to me. Therefore go and make disciples of all nations, baptizing them in the name of the Father and of the Son and of the Holy Spirit, and teaching them to obey everything I have commanded you. And surely I am with you always, to the very end of the age." (Matthew 28:18–20 NIV)

Some thoughts come to mind when I read these final words Jesus spoke. Have you ever said goodbye to someone you love who you will not see for a long time? Usually the last words you say to each other are significant and something you want to remember. What if the disciples did not pay attention to what Jesus was telling them? What if they had not walked in the power and authority He gave them and had not done what Jesus asked them to do? If this had been the case, I don't think you and I would be having this conversation right now. It's quite miraculous when you think about it—how God worked in and through these men who gave up their lives to tell people about the freedom found only in Jesus, which has transformed billions of peoples' lives and this world for eternity.

In my own life, the gap I needed to close was connected to my desire to have a closer and deeper relationship with God. In the pursuit, I discovered there was freedom available to me that I did not know I did not have. I asked God for help, and Jesus healed me and set me free from a bunch of stuff. All very good. But to draw nearer to God, I needed to look closely at our relationship itself. I had asked Jesus to be my Lord and Savior long ago. Yes, He saved me, but had I really made him Lord of my life? This narrowed gap—where I say, yes, Lord, I'm open and available to do whatever you ask and whatever it takes to go where you ask me to go—Dr. Murray calls it the signing of the blank page, where I say, "Lord, anytime, anywhere, and anything—first I sign the blank page, and then you, Lord, fill in the rest of the details for me."

Jesus challenged the disciples on this important gap that I personally needed to close. Here's more insight. This parable of the wise and foolish builders is a favorite bedtime story in our family—

> "So why do you keep calling me 'Lord, Lord!' when you don't do what I say? I will show you what it's like when someone comes to me, listens to my teaching, and then follows it. It is like a person building a house who digs deep and lays the foundation on solid rock. When the floodwaters rise and break against that house, it stands firm because it is well built. But anyone who hears and doesn't obey is like a person who builds a house without a foundation. When the floods sweep down against that house, it will collapse into a heap of ruins." (Luke 6:46–49 NLT)

I'm thankful the disciples wrestled with their faith and made the decision to sign the blank page and do what Jesus asked them to do. They followed Jesus. They were empowered and walked in God's resurrection power and authority and impacted and influenced the world in an exponential way because of it. They shared their story of what they had seen and heard. They gave up everything to be part of God's plan. They knew and believed Jesus and that He is worthy of all their praise. Jesus told them, "You call me 'Teacher' and 'Lord,' and rightly so, for that is what I am." (John 13:13 NIV)

We've come full circle. Remember I mentioned I like connecting with missionaries and how much I love important assignments? I've discovered it starts not with the assignment but with Jesus—and in my case, making Him truly the Lord of my life. I know He is who He says He is and that He is worthy of all my thankfulness and praise.

I have to be honest with you; this has been one of my least favorite chapters to write. Sometimes I just don't want to go there—to those places where I need to take a step back and work on these areas. And what if I've already done a bunch of work? Is there really more? Why can't I just get on with helping others and my calling in life—do I really need to take time to close my gaps?

How about you? What are some gaps in your life you need to close? Remember—free people can help free people.

To be a Truth Teller, you need to know the truth.

To be a Freedom Fighter, you need to be free.

You can't give what you do not possess.

You can't help people if you've not been helped.

You can't coach people if you've not been coached.

You can't lead people if you have not been led.

You can't teach people what you've not learned yourself.

You can't help to free people if you are not free.

You can do this. You are doing this. Close one gap at a time. Deal with what's right in front of you and standing in the way of what God has for you next. And in the waiting, know that Jesus is your advocate and loves you and is standing in the gap for you. I believe in you. I'm praying for you. Just keep going.

YOU SACRED TIME, SPACE, AND CALLING

15-MINUTE FREEDOM EXERCISE

My number one pet peeve is negativity. I attribute it to being a glass is half full kind of person or looking for the positives in people and situations. But I've also been negative myself, and when that happens, I really don't like myself in these scenarios. I was challenged by one of my mentors to dig a little deeper as to why it bothered me so much. What I came up with is that when someone is negative, they tend to be focused on themselves. And then as I took this a step further, if I'm negative and I'm focused on myself, then I don't have the capacity to be present. Wow! And guess what one of my most important values is? Being present! When I'm negative or someone around me is negative, it takes away from being present—in the moment—and as a person of faith, it takes away from what God intends for that time.

Take some time to think about what bothers you. Do you have any pet peeves?

_____

_____

_____

What do you think is the reason you are bothered by what you just wrote?

_____

_____

_____

I continue to be challenged in this area. I make it a regular practice to sit and journal and ask, "God, what are you saying to me through the way I'm feeling about this negative situation?" I'm learning that negativity in itself is not bad; in fact, it's something that if we respond to it in a healthy way, can help identity an area of our lives where God wants to offer us more freedom. I think when we experience negativity or negative emotions or feelings, it's God's way of getting our attention—telling us there's something going on inside and there's more freedom that He has for us. I'm thankful for the mentors in my life who have encouraged me to take these negative feelings to God and ask Him what He wants to say to me through the way I'm feeling. There's a healing that takes place when we give God the opportunity to speak into our situation. We can't stay in the negative, but at the same time, we don't want to miss what we can learn from it. Please take some time to journal or write below your thoughts and feelings on what I've shared.

_____

_____

_____

SPECIAL TIME WITH GOD
Set aside 15 minutes. Read **PSALM 51** in the Old Testament. You may consider reading it a second time out loud. What verse sticks out or connects with you? Apply the SOAP Method.

S – Scripture – Write out the verse you chose. Write it in this space below or in your journal.

_____

_____

O – Observation – What are one or two facts that you observe from the verse you chose?

_____

_____

A – Application – How can you personally apply this verse to your life?

_____

_____

P – Prayer – Write out a prayer to God related to your reading today. There is no right or wrong way to do this. Prayer is having a conversation with God. Think of this as a conversation starter between you and God.

_____

_____

_____

PRAYER AND ENCOURAGEMENT

"**Be Still**, and **know**" (Psalm 46:10). When we **listen** with our hearts, we **learn** a lot.

I hope you've had an opportunity to try out the SOAP Bible Study Method. Spending time in God's Word changes you from the inside out. If this is something new to you or you've not read the Bible in a while, I encourage you to push through what may seem a bit awkward, open a Bible, and be open to what God has for you today. Being in God's word—reading it for yourself and applying it to your life—is where real transformation happens. This is where the Bible talks about being transformed by the renewing of your mind (Romans 12:2). When we read and study God's Word, we not only receive the wisdom and truth meant for us but there is a rewiring that takes place through the power of God's words as seeds of truth are being sown in our hearts on a regular basis.

Pray! Take some time when you read your Bible to pray and ask God to help you prepare your heart to spend time with Him and enjoy the benefit of His presence with you. Confess your sins, and keep short accounts with God. Pray and ask the Holy Spirit to move freely in your life and highlight the wisdom and truths God has for you. Ask for God's wisdom, direction, and next steps for you. Know that God sees you, loves you, cares for you, and can't wait to spend time with you.

10

WORTH IT TO PURSUE

"If you ever seem to be sliding back into the very thing you've
already been set free of, don't even waste time getting discouraged.
Often what seems like the same old thing coming back again may
be a new layer surfacing that needs to come off. You're not going
backwards—you are going deeper."

STORMIE OMARTIAN, *THE POWER OF A PRAYING WOMAN*

W HEN I SET out to write this book, my purpose was to share my story
and how God has brought perspective, wholeness, and freedom to my
life. My hope has been that in telling my story, it would bring encouragement
and hope to others.

The book writing experience has turned out to be much more than I
expected. Writing in itself has been a healing process, and it is here, in these
pages, that I'm finding my writer's voice. I'm thankful for this opportunity
as I'm connecting the dots in God's big story and seeing more of Him in my

story. My new hope is that through telling my story, you are inspired to find your voice and share your story with the world around you.

The decision to Break the Cycle of Hurt resulted in a major shift in my life. Leadership expert John C. Maxwell says, "Everything begins with a decision. Then, we have to manage that decision for the rest of your life."[1] Yes, most definitely this is a rest of my life decision. The past seven years have shown my commitment to this cause.

And so, as I've been writing and planning to share with you about my journey and how the cycles of hurt, pain, defeat, and lies were keeping me stuck, caged, and imprisoned, something unspeakable happened! In the process of telling my story, I shared before that I found myself HURT AGAIN—and not just once but twice!

I'm talking about the kind of hurt that blindsides you. Not just minor scrapes but gunshot wounds. One hurt came through an important relationship where trust had been broken. Another was from an administrative position where I felt unheard and overwhelmed by something I was not comfortable doing.

And so in the middle of sharing with you how God healed me in the past, I unexpectedly found myself needing to go through the exact process that I wanted to share and encourage others with through my story. In fact, I actually started to question everything to that point. I wondered, *Will all the work that I've done in the past be for nothing? Will it all be lost?* This was not a place I would have chosen to be.

Close to these fresh wounds stood familiar and unwanted feelings of bitterness, anger, and resentment. These negative emotions felt trapped inside, and they overwhelmed my days—my heart broken, spirit crushed, and emotions stretched to the point where I felt physically not well and weakened at my core. But I thought that I had been set free from this stuff! What now? Have you ever been in a place like this? Have you ever questioned the progress you have made?

At this same time, I had a trip planned to join my mastermind group (an accountability group of like-minded individuals committed to personal growth and development) in Ohio. It had been scheduled for months, and I did not want to miss this opportunity. I felt so weak and had no strength. I was close to canceling my trip and heard the words from a favorite song, called "Cornerstone": "Weak made strong in the Savior's love. Through the storm, He is Lord, Lord of all."

This passage in the Bible encourages me every time I read it. In 2 Corinthians 12:9–11 (NIV), it says "But he said to me, 'My grace is sufficient for you, for my power is made perfect in weakness.' Therefore I will boast all the more gladly about my weaknesses, so that Christ's power may rest on me. That is why, for Christ's sake, I delight in weaknesses, in insults, in hardships, in persecutions, in difficulties. For when I am weak, then I am strong."

God met me in my hurts, weakness, and struggle. In fact, He met me in a prison, as you will see as I share both literally and figuratively.

It is a miracle how I made it to Ohio and back. I'm thankful for a strength that was not my own that made a way for me to go and see what God had in store. It seemed quite fitting that our first stop would be a prison. The purpose of our two-day meeting was to walk away with a plan to go from our day job to our dream job. But first we needed to find out if there was anything getting in our way of making this a reality.

On our first day in Ohio, we went to Shawshank Prison, where the Academy Award-nominated movie, *Shawshank Redemption*, was filmed. I literally sat in a prison cell, which is ironic because trapped is how I was feeling about the negative feelings compounding inside of me. It was a time when the hurts were still surfacing and the light of hope seemed dimly lit.

A place in the Bible where God has often met me is in the Book of Isaiah. I actually get a kick out of the ways that He gets my attention through this freedom-fighting book. Here, written over seven hundred years before Jesus came to earth, is where we learn about His mission and purpose for coming to rescue the lost. In the past, I had been the worst kind of captive—specifically, one who did not know I needed freedom.

I've learned that Jesus came to set someone like me free.

He came for someone like me, who needed to hear some good news.

He came for someone like me, who needed someone to care for my crushed and broken heart.

He came for someone like me, who needed my mourning replaced with joy, my despair replaced with praise.

Isaiah 61:1–3 (NIV) talks about Jesus and why He came for you and me—

> "The Spirit of the Sovereign LORD is on me, because the LORD has anointed me to proclaim good news to the poor. He has sent me to bind up the brokenhearted, to proclaim freedom for the captives and release from darkness for the prisoners, to proclaim the year of the LORD's favor and the day of vengeance of our God, to comfort all who mourn, and provide for those who grieve in Zion— to bestow on them a crown of beauty instead of ashes, the oil of joy instead of mourning, and a garment of praise instead of a spirit of despair. They will be called oaks of righteousness, a planting of the LORD for the display of his splendor."

At Shawshank, my most memorable experience turned out to be when we had the opportunity to sit in our own prison cell for a time of personal reflection. My coach, Kary, prepared a handout and had some great questions for us to consider.

From my prison cell, I could hear birds outside—singing and free.

I wanted to sing and be free.

As I looked around, what could I see?

In front of me, I saw steel bars, chipped paint, dirty windows, rust, dirt, dust, broken furniture, and a mirror so warped you couldn't see yourself in it.

At times it was difficult to see anything with the reflection of light on walls through the bars from the outside windows—and yet I saw a beam of light shining through. I felt the warmth of the sun as it met me in this dark cell.

I turned my attention to the next question: What could I hear?

More birds, people walking, people talking, people coughing, papers moving, silence, my feet moving, and quiet.

The sound of the birds outside could be hopeful, or when you feel like you are locked in a prison or a cage, it could drive you absolutely crazy.

And then, what did I feel?

In these surroundings, I felt cold, damp, despair, fear, anxiety, and hopelessness.

I stood and held the bars of my prison cell—they were cold, damp, and rigid. The bars felt like my hurt feelings inside, symbolizing the feeling of being trapped, caged, voiceless, scared, and hopeless.

And yet, as I stood there, I could feel air coming through the bars. I felt a slight breeze. The word that quickly came to mind—HOPE. I wondered, *Could it be hope coming through the bars to meet me?*

As I stood there, I asked myself, what do these bars represent? Broken relationships? My hurt circumstances? My self-limiting beliefs?

I found myself kneeling by the bed in the cell. I know, what was I thinking? The floor felt cold and hard under my knees. I could not see the floor surface through the dirt, and the condition of the mattress was even worse. There was nothing I wanted to touch. For some reason, I kept looking at the toilet and the sink; the thought of going to the bathroom there was horrifying. Thankfully, I did not need to go.

I thought of the prisoners who once resided in this place and how this must have stripped them of all remaining dignity. I thought that this is what the enemy wants us to think about ourselves when we find ourselves trapped in our failures, fears, hurts, and circumstances of life. This is the enemy's dirty, lying plan—please know that this is not God's plan. Jesus came to set the captives free and heal broken hearts. He did not come to step on our pain; He came to rescue us and care for our broken hearts. He came because He loves us and was willing to do what He needed to do to set us free.

I'm on my knees, Lord. I give these negative feelings to you—
Anger
Bitterness
Resentment
Fear of failure
Fear of success
What would you say to me through what I'm feeling? What lies am I believing that are trapped inside of me?
I'm overwhelmed. Please help me.

I sat and waited to hear from the Creator of Heaven and Earth. What I sensed God saying to me were not words in an audible voice but thoughts, lies, and self-limiting beliefs that were coming to mind. I could barely write them down. It seemed the lies came from a place deep inside that did not want me to be free from them.

Can I share them with you? These thoughts are in the context of me personally and where I was at the time.

You're not good enough.
What do you have to offer?
Your ideas have been done before.
You can't have the marriage you want.
You are not smart enough.
Family relationships in your life will never change.
Family relationships in your life are lost.
There is no hope.
You can't do this.
Your heritage is not godly enough.
You don't have the education you need.
You can't have a healed marriage.

I felt the tears roll down my face. Remembering that God's words are convicting, loving, kind, and helpful, I knew these accusing words were not from Him. I knew these lies were keeping me trapped inside.

Sitting on a broken bed in a cold prison cell, I went on to write more—

Lord, in my relationships, am I in the way of how you want to restore them? Are my emotions and response to them getting in the way?

Am I the prison bars?

Am I the obstacle?

Lord, what I'd like to do is leave ALL that is holding me back here in this cell. I'm thinking about the people who resided here as long as they did. The lost hopes and dreams that died in here. The people who may not have known your great love for them.

How can one not engage in a conversation with you, Lord? There is no hiding that can be done here. A prison cell is a place where you can find out that the war and the enemy that a person thinks is on the outside is actually on the inside. When all their circumstances and relationships are removed from the picture, a person is left here in this cell with themselves…and you, Lord.

Shine your light in the darkness of my life—no more hiding of any kind. Lord, I do not want these lies and self-limiting beliefs in my life. If there are more, please show me. Maybe not today, because this is about all I can handle today. Another day, okay?

Please take and break these lies in my life. Can I leave them in the prison cell?

Lord, what do you want to say to me now? What is the truth that you intend for me to hear? Please speak life, hope, and encouragement over me. Please break these lies, Lord, and replace them with your healing truth.

I then waited in my overwhelmed state. Some thoughts came to mind. Again, all in the context of me personally and if I can share what I sensed God impressing on my heart.

You are a Truth Teller.

You inspire and encourage others to pursue more and not miss what is intended for them.

Kim, you are chosen, you are called, and you are part of a royal priesthood— my child who I have chosen to do great things for my kingdom.

You can say freely…

I am a Truth Teller.

I am a Freedom Fighter.

I have everything I need to do what God is asking me to do.

I can walk in the freedom and confidence that God has a plan and a purpose to heal and fully restore my marriage and for it to be all He intends it to be.

God has a plan to reconcile family relationships in my life. He has a plan for the people I care about.

My unique message needs to be heard.

I am smart enough. I am enough.

I have a story and a message the world needs to hear.

I felt a release, like something inside of me was being healed and renewed. I could see clearly how I could leave the resentment, bitterness, and anger behind. And I felt a willingness to begin the forgiveness process towards those who hurt me—and leave ALL that was holding me back IN THE PRISON CELL with Jesus, who came to set me free from all this.

Later my coach asked us to write a letter to ourselves and seal it, and he would send it back to us toward the end of the year. The letter, which I had forgotten about, arrived in the mail months later. On the back of the envelope, my coach wrote, "I believe in you." I thought back to a time when I was thankful to have borrowed his belief in me. Thankfully, these words found me in a place of greater strength and perspective. I had experienced more God-given freedom and healing on the inside.

It can be kind of awkward writing a letter to yourself. Anyway, here are the words I wrote—

Dear Kim,

It's okay. You are going to walk out free.

You are free. Leave this all in the prison cell.

You can walk free NOW.

Jesus died for you. He sat in the prison cell for you. He paid the price for you.

You are connected to Christ, your calling, and your community.

As each hurt, obstacle, mess, or lie comes to stand in your way, deal with it—one at a time. Keep asking for help. You are moving closer to the BIG DREAM that God has given you. Be encouraged. Keep going.

It doesn't have to be perfect. Hang on to Jesus. Cling to Him because He is your Hope. You've got this.

Love,

Kim

As a Deeper Path coach, I share with clients the OPUS framework (I share more on this in Chapter 13), which was designed by my coach, Kary Oberbrunner, and his coach and builder, Chet Scott. I referred earlier to my BIG DREAM—this is something that I have the privilege of helping others identify in their own lives. Some people know what they want, and all they need is a framework to make their vision a reality. Some have forgotten how to dream, and it's so exciting to see them explore the possibilities and come alive again. In either case, I think no matter where we are, we are all challenged to go deeper and discover more about WHO and WHY we were created to be.

At the same time, when we are thinking about a dream we have for our lives, our minds can quickly jump to the barriers that would prevent us from making it a reality. Has this ever happened to you? This is crucial to pay attention to—we need to be prepared to fight against the lies and for this overarching vision for our lives.

Within the Deeper Path coaching model, we talk about our WHY being our purpose for being on this earth. We also talk about our WHY being our "crown." Examples of some obstacles or lies you may encounter are "You are not good enough" or "You do not have the resources or the relationships to make this dream a reality." Expect it. This is called resistance, and it's not going anywhere if you are pursuing something that is significant to you. Keep moving. The freedom God has for you and the BIG DREAM He has placed on your heart are worth pursuing.

In some respects, we can look at the obstacles as a catalyst to move us forward. I think most people want to see movement and growth in their lives and not stay where they are, which shows how necessary it is to overcome the hindrances that come our way.

Resistance tells us we are heading in the right direction and to keep going. What we really want to avoid is getting stuck in the resistance, which can manifest into a pit. Expanding on this further, if you think of your dream or vision for your life (or your WHY) as your crown, let's consider the difficulties that you face as your daily cross. You may have heard "pick up your cross daily." This is derived from Luke 9:23 (NIV), where Jesus declared, "Whoever wants to be my disciple must deny themselves and take up their cross daily and follow me."

I think the only way we can successfully take up our cross daily is by keeping our eyes on the One who wears the Victor's Crown—the One who has overcome all obstacles. I felt confident I could leave my hurt and the lies I believed back in the Shawshank prison cell because of the finished work of Jesus. And I could walk out of the prison cell with my head high and with the truth and the power of Jesus and all that He came to this earth to do for you and for me. It's because of Jesus that I can pick up my cross and overcome what's in front of me and I can focus on my crown, my WHY—the dream He's given me.

It wasn't that the hurt had gone away or that my circumstances had changed. It's that I had placed what I could not carry any longer with Jesus so that I could begin the healing process. The burdens I felt moved from my shoulders to Jesus's shoulders. It made all the difference.

A year has passed since I left Shawshank. God has provided much more clarity, healing, and redemption on the other side of trusting Him in that prison cell. It's now been seven years since I decided to Break the Cycle of Hurt. Seven years of prayer, fighting for freedom, pushing through, speaking the truth in love, pursuing healing and forgiveness, asking for help at every corner, getting in the way, getting out of the way, and running this faith-filled race. I've seen mercy and grace in the failing. I've felt God's unconditional love in all circumstances. The breakthroughs I've experienced and the miracles I've seen are thankfully too many to count—and all for God's glory.

This last year, the enemy tried to tell me that all was lost and that all the healing work that had been done was gone—like poof!

Well, that's NOT true. I don't accept it!

Jesus, my Lord and Savior, says no—this is NOT the end—this pain and hurt is not the end. You are faithful. Be faithful and keep going. Your time is coming. I'm working behind the scenes. More healing and restoration is coming. Be open. You've been faithful to do the work. Keep going. There's more to be done. Be open. Miracles are coming. Just keep going. Your freedom is worth it to pursue.

I'm taking authority and standing up. How about you? Jesus said, "It is finished."[2] This is how I could leave my anger, resentment, bitterness, and fear of failure with Him in the prison cell. He came to this earth to mend our broken hearts and take away what keeps us from being free. What would you like to ask Jesus to take from you? The freedom He offers is worth pursuing as you stand and fight from His place of victory. May this be a source of encouragement to you—

"I have fought the good fight, I have finished the race, and I have remained faithful. And now the prize awaits me—the crown of righteousness, which the Lord, the righteous Judge, will give me on the day of his return. And the prize is not just for me but for all who eagerly look forward to his appearing." (2 Timothy 4:7–8 NLT)

"The LORD will fight for you; you need only to be still." (Exodus 14:14 NIV)

YOUR SACRED TIME, SPACE, AND CALLING

15-MINUTE FREEDOM EXERCISE

The lies we believe about ourselves or our life circumstances can hold us back. "I am not enough" or "I don't have enough" can be the excuses we tell ourselves. These lies can keep us from living out our life's purpose and our BIG DREAM. If you know Jesus, because of His finished work on the cross, we are enough and we have enough. The truth is, you might be your biggest obstacle. I know I was mine.

What dream, goal, circumstance, or possibility in a relationship have you hoped to see materialize or see changes in over the past year? (This is something you think about every day. You may be making progress, or you may not be getting anywhere.)

Write it down.

_____
_____
_____
_____
_____

What are some obstacles, self-limiting beliefs, or lies that have been holding you back from becoming the person you have been created to be?

_____
_____
_____

Would you be willing to ask God to reveal His truth to you and help you overcome these barriers?

_____
_____
_____

(I've provided a space under "Prayer and Encouragement" in this chapter to carry on this conversation.)

SPECIAL TIME WITH GOD

Set aside 15 minutes. Read **PSALM 142** in the Old Testament. You may consider reading it a second time out loud. What verse sticks out or connects with you? Apply the SOAP Method.

S – Scripture – Write out the verse you chose. Write it in this space below or in your journal.

_____

_____

_____

O – Observation – What are one or two facts that you observe from the verse you chose?

_____

_____

_____

A – Application – How can you personally apply this verse to your life?

_____

_____

_____

P – Prayer – Write out a prayer to God related to your reading today. There is no right or wrong way to do this. Prayer is having a conversation with God. Think of this as a conversation starter between you and God.

_____

_____

_____

PRAYER AND ENCOURAGEMENT

Try this strategy. Think of all the obstacles that you see that are getting in the way of your dream or goal that you just wrote down in the 15-Minute Freedom Exercise. Write down everything that comes to mind. Write them in point form at first, and then go back and expand on them in your journal if you need to.

1._____   12._____
2._____   13._____
3._____   14._____
4._____   15._____
5._____   16._____
6._____   17._____
7._____   18._____
8._____   19._____
9._____   20._____
10._____   21._____
11._____

Pray! Consider giving these obstacles to God. Say, "God, I give these roadblocks to you. Please help me, give me wisdom, and lead and guide me through them." If God has placed a dream or desire on your heart, He wants you to see it become a reality. He wants to help you. Because of God, all things are possible. Ask the Holy Spirit to show you how to overcome these obstacles. Ask God to make it clear what is your part and what you are to leave with Him to orchestrate. Ask Him for forgiveness where you need to. Ask yourself some honest questions. Are you your biggest obstacle? Are you getting in the way of what God wants to do in your life? You may be tired and want to give up. Don't! The fact that there is resistance and perceived obstacles is a good thing. Lean in to them. Plug in to God's power source, not yours— or any other source for that matter. God's ways are higher. Obstacles are not in God's vocabulary. All things are possible with God and beyond what you could ever imagine.[3]

PART III—FREE

"For to be free is not merely to cast off one's chains, but to live in a way that respects and enhances the freedom of others."

NELSON MANDELA, *LONG WALK TO FREEDOM*

YOU KEEP DOING the work. You see miracles and glimpses of freedom along the way. You are becoming the person you were created and are called to be. You are breaking free from the pain and hurts inside. You are living a life of intention and changing the world around you.

The cage is open. You have the option to be free. Free people discover they can help free people.

You are connected to a Love calling your name. You are singing your freedom song—you are sharing your passion and story with the world that needs you.

11

THE OTHER SIDE

"It is for freedom that Christ has set us free. Stand firm, then, and
do not let yourselves be burdened again by a yoke of slavery."

(GALATIANS 5:1 NIV)

MY WORLD HAS been rocked these last number of months. It's been in the making for a long time. I actually prayed for this to take place. Well, I prayed for it to happen to someone else, not me. At this point in my healing journey, I thought someone else needed their perspective changed, not me. Well, God had something else in mind.

But I've done this already.

I've gone for help. I've shared my story.

I've received the healing.

I've experienced the freedom.

I've even helped others on their healing and freedom journey.

Do I really need to take time away from my purpose, calling, and even writing this book to do this?

God, please fix the other person, and all my problems will be solved.

Oh my goodness, how did I not see this coming? I had thought the freedom God gave me in the past was more than I could have ever imagined. I guess I also thought this would be it for me personally and that I'd go on living out my purpose of helping others find freedom. How short sighted had I been? How prideful could I be? Don't get me wrong; I'm incredibly thankful for the God-given freedom I have experienced. The truth is, I don't ever want to forget to sing God's praises for all that He's done for me and my family.

And so my kicking and screaming session with God continued—

Do I really need to go back and do more work?

With a gentle and loving response, I sensed God impressing on my heart two words—*Be Open*. I knew then I needed to take this step, and so I waited patiently for what God had in store.

Thinking back to my question—can one person change and make a difference if everything around them stays the same? I'm incredibly thankful the outcome is a resounding YES. And the choice to pursue freedom has yielded an unexpected and positive ripple effect in the lives of the people I care about. With God's help, I'm learning how to break free from the hurts inside and change the world around me.

It's important to note that freedom is not a quick fix or a one-time event. I've seen and heard from people who have been miraculously set free from sickness and oppression in an instant. For me personally, my journey to wholeness has been and continues to be a process.

Freedom is a marathon, not a sprint.

Hebrews 12:1–2 (NIV) says, "Therefore, since we are surrounded by such a great cloud of witnesses, let us throw off everything that hinders and the sin that so easily entangles. And let us run with perseverance the race marked out for us, fixing our eyes on Jesus, the pioneer and perfecter of faith. For the joy set before him he endured the cross, scorning its shame, and sat down at the right hand of the throne of God."

So in these last few months, God's given me a whole new perspective on how much He loves us and wants to care for our hearts and heal them— MORE healing and even more freedom that I did not know I did not have.

I now see people and their hearts differently. I see the pain and the hurt in the world differently. This fresh, new, world-rocking point of view has interrupted my thinking and forever changed me—again!

I can't imagine what God will do the next time.

Where are you on your freedom journey? If you've already experienced God-given freedom, could there be more for you on the other side? Is there a hurt or a wound that may not have been fully healed in the past that you may need to go back to? Don't do this alone. Be sure to ask others for help and prayer.

If you find yourself at a low point in your life, know that God is with you in the valley. He's not forgotten about you. I don't think He wastes our pain. God is working behind the scenes toward a greater purpose in your life beyond these desert times.

Have you ever wondered what it is like on the other side of freedom? It was not something I had thought about. I was really not aware of the possibilities. What I've learned and keep learning is that with awareness comes the possibly for hope, healing, and freedom. The truth is, these were opportunities available to me that I did not know I did not have. When I decided to break free from hurts and chronic pain in my life, this turned out to be a defining moment and a catalyst that has led to genuine wholeness and healing in my life. Here's what I've discovered to be on "The Other Side"—

The Other Side of Freedom by Kim Gowdy

On the other side of freedom is someone rescued and saved by Grace and freed from the addiction and pit of people pleasing and performance-based living.

On the other side of freedom is someone with healed emotional wounds that don't hurt any more so people can see their Redeemer healed them.

On the other side of freedom is someone radically transformed who yet continues to be a work in progress fully motivated by Grace, Mercy, and Love.

On the other side of freedom is a Freedom Fighter who has been rescued and now given a heart for the lost and oppressed and who believes in the power of prayer and the FREEDOM that only God can give.

On the other side of freedom is a Truth Teller who has been lovingly set free from the pain, hurt, and lies they believed about themselves and now deeply desires this same life-giving freedom for others.

On the other side of freedom is someone who knows where to go when they are overwhelmed and on empty—to a loving and caring Savior who is the only One who can fill their love tank, lift their heavy burdens, and give them true REST for their soul.

On the other side of freedom is someone who could not have done this without their Lord and Savior, an authentic faith community, Truth Tellers, Freedom Fighters, and friends and family who loved, prayed, supported, invested, and poured into them.

On the other side of freedom is someone who is FREE to be themselves in all situations, FREE to love, and FREE to be loved.

On the other side of freedom is someone who has found a voice for their story and is courageously sharing and encouraging others to do the same.

On the other side of freedom is someone with newfound PASSION and PURPOSE for life.

On the other side of freedom is someone with a new song of HOPE in their heart.

On the other side of freedom is someone with a God-given BIG DREAM to pursue.

On the other side of freedom is someone who is open to receiving MORE freedom and then more PASSION, PURPOSE, HOPE, and VISION on the other side.

That someone is me. On the other side, I am FREE.

That someone may or can be you too!

I knew at the beginning of my decision to follow after freedom and wholeness that there would be hope and healing available. What I did not know is that on the other side would be a dream God had for me.

If I may share with you my song of hope—my BIG DREAM...

I have a dream to be a part of something bigger than myself. I am a Freedom Fighter. I am a Truth Teller. I have a heart for the lost. I am living loved and sharing this LOVE so graciously given to me with my husband, my kids, family, friends, those who know Jesus, and those who don't.

I have a dream I am leading, encouraging, and supporting people as they discover the freedom in knowing who they are and why they were created to be. I am passionate about learning, writing, creating processes/workshops, coaching, and hosting events in my community. I am part of a team of people pioneering and leading organizations in Canada and around the world.

I have a dream I'm sitting down for an intentional time of writing and reflection. I just finished a book I wrote for my kids and others about my incredible journey to freedom, healing, and wholeness.

I am in awe of what God is doing. I so enjoy connecting the dots and seeing how God is moving in people's lives. I have a heart for connecting people to genuine community and others who know and love Jesus. I am living my heart's desire of sharing the gospel with people—meeting them where they are and introducing them to the Love of their life.

I have a dream I am intentional in my relationships with God, my husband, my kids, family, and close friends. We spend time together. It's booked in the calendar. These relationships are deepening, and we are getting to know each other more and more.

As I am encouraging my husband and reflecting back on a promise God gave me that has come to fruition, I'm in awe of what this all means and the freedom that has come to many people as a result.

I have a dream my kids know Jesus. They hear His voice clearly. They are fully devoted to Him. They know they are secure, accepted, and loved. They know their unique passion and purpose in life, and they are living it.

I have a dream I am active and healthy. My life is clutter- and mess-free, and I am living my God-given passion and purpose. I am continuing to choose the great things from the many good things. I am honoring my values. I am singing my song—the one that was given to me. My life is rich and full, and I am thankful.

Tomorrow I'm going to a friend's house for coffee. She is what I would call a "prayer warrior." Five years ago, I remember going to meet this same friend, whom I didn't know as well at the time.

On the way, I sensed God's Spirit whispering to me, "I'm teaching you how to pray." And now, when I look back, wow, I had no idea what would be coming.

I'm eternally grateful for this now dear friend and how she has faithfully prayed for me and my family—and really has come alongside and mentored me in becoming a prayer warrior too. I love that God chose us to be friends in this time and place in history.

I also just love God's sense of humor when I think about how I grew up in a church environment where we didn't independently pray out loud. We sat quietly in our pews and had times where we all read a prayer or had a time of reflection and silent prayer, and for the most part, only the minister prayed out loud.

At our current church, I remember attending a women's retreat a number of years ago, and a friend asked me if I would consider praying with women as part of a prayer team. I felt terrified at the thought and did not feel equipped to do this. I responded yes despite my feelings and prayed afraid, relying on God to guide my conversation as I sat with each woman.

It's funny because I'm going to the same women's retreat this spring, and I'm now leading that same prayer team. I share this only because honestly, if God can use someone like me who was once scared to pray out loud with people, He can use you to do what He is calling you to do.

God is in the business of equipping those He calls.

Like God does, I believe in you.

In the waiting for freedom or more freedom that God has for you, remember how He is equipping you.

In my own life, I've found the secret weapon in the fight is prayer. Another is spending time with God reading the Bible—the SOAP Method I share is an amazing tool to add to your devotional tool box. It effectively combines discovering God's Word for yourself and prayer!

A book that helped me tremendously is Beth Moore's *Breaking Free: Discover the Victory of Total Surrender.* She has a well-known Bible study of the same name that I had the privilege to co-lead a beautiful group of women through with a good friend of mine. On the need for prayer in our lives, Beth writes, "What victory the enemy has in winning us over to prayerlessness! He would rather we do anything than pray. He'd rather see us serve ourselves into the ground because he knows we'll eventually grow resentful without prayer. He'd rather see us study the Bible into the wee hours of the morning, because he knows we'll never have deep understanding and power to live what we've learned without prayer. He knows prayerless lives are powerless lives, while prayerful lives are powerful lives!"[1]

It's important to remember that in tough times how God is teaching you to pray and equipping you to fight. I've highlighted in the devotional section of my *The Daily Walk Bible,* these wise words: "Have you ever tried to hammer a nail with your shoe? Or tighten a screw with a fingernail? Or shield yourself from a rainstorm with just a newspaper? When you need a hammer or screwdriver or umbrella, nothing else will do. Are you living your spiritual life that way, using shoes for hammers and newspapers for umbrellas? God has provided the implements necessary for successful Christian living, but perhaps you have tried to make do by substituting your own tools and plans."[2] Ephesians 6:10–18 may or may not be familiar to you—read it with a new sense of urgency today:

> "A final word: Be strong in the Lord and in his mighty power. Put on all of God's armor so that you will be able to stand firm against all strategies of the devil. For we are not fighting against flesh-and-blood enemies, but against evil rulers and authorities of the unseen world, against mighty powers in this dark world, and against evil spirits in the heavenly places. Therefore, put on every piece of God's armor so you will be able to resist the enemy in the time of evil. Then after the battle you will still be standing firm. Stand your ground, putting on the belt of truth and the body armor of God's righteousness. For shoes, put on the peace that comes from the Good News so that you will be fully prepared. In addition to all of these, hold up the shield of faith to stop the fiery arrows of the devil. Put on salvation as your helmet, and take the sword of the Spirit, which is the word of God. Pray in the Spirit at all times and on every occasion. Stay alert and be persistent in your prayers for all believers everywhere." (Ephesians 6:10–18 NLT)

One of my prayer mentors from afar is Stormie Omartian. I've read many of her books (*The Power of a Praying Wife* and *The Power of a Praying Parent* are two in particular I've read and refer to again and again.) and have found her prayers to be helpful in praying for my family and even myself. If you are not sure what to pray, she teaches you how to effectively pray for the people you care about and, more importantly, through the power of God's Word. She shared this post on social media: "The armor of God is not something we put on and then go hide under the bed. We put it on not only for defensive but offensive purposes as well. While it's true that the battle has already been won against the enemy—because of what Jesus did on the cross—that doesn't mean we do nothing. We have to exhibit strong faith in God and His Word, and we have to pray aggressively without backing down."[3]

I've talked about becoming a Freedom Fighter and now a Prayer Warrior—so what do I mean by fighting? It's not a punching someone out or hitting them back when they hit you kind of thing. It's not getting your back up when someone hurts or offends you or getting even with them. No, it's not that kind of fight. As Stormie Omartian shares in *The Power of a Praying Woman Bible*, "The battle for our lives, and the lives and souls of our children, our husbands, our friends, our families, our neighbors, and our nation is waged on our knees. When we don't pray, it's like sitting on the sidelines watching those we love and care about scrambling through a war zone, getting shot at from every angle. When we do pray, however, we're in the battle alongside them, approaching God's power on their behalf. If we also declare the Word of God in our prayers, then we wield a powerful weapon against which no enemy can prevail."[4]

I've been in that "prayerless" warzone she's talking about. How about you? In my mind, freedom fighting is surrendering the battle to God and His power, knowing that He has fought for us and is in control of all things. It's also understanding that I have a role to play in this bigger story. My part is trusting and praising God for all He's done, recognizing there is a battle, being faithful to do what God is asking me to do, walking in the freedom He has given me, and staying connected to my Creator, Core, and Community. Spending time with God, prayer, studying God's Word, and praying God's Word make me the most effective Freedom Fighter and Prayer Warrior in this fight.

Yes, I realize not everyone prays or thinks about prayer as often as I do. However, as followers of Christ, we are all called to pray and talk to our Father in Heaven, to pray defensively and offensively, and to take a stand against the enemy's schemes.

As I've shared with you, I like to say my faith and my two-way conversations with God are how I live and breathe. The armor of God is something I aim to pray each day for myself and my family. I ask God to equip us for the battle and clothe us with:

The Helmet of Salvation—thanking God for all He's done and for saving us.

The Belt of Truth tied tightly to keep God's truth in and the enemy's lies out of our lives.

The Breastplate of Righteousness—asking God to make us discerning about right and wrong decisions.

The Sword of the Spirit, which represents the Word of God—asking God to give us a thirst and a hunger for His Word.

The Shield of Faith—asking God to protect us from the attacks of the enemy.

The Shoes of the Gospel of Peace on our feet to take us into every situation.

I'll share more about a helpful way to pray God's Word for you and your loved ones in the prayer and encouragement section. I'd love for the opportunity to share with you more about prayer and prayer strategies outside of this book.

Your freedom is worth fighting for and pursuing. Your potential and purpose are on the other side of your perseverance. More freedom is on the other side. You're not alone, and you don't need to be afraid. Fight with faith and not fear. Remember, God is with you at each step—He's fighting for you. And remember how He is equipping you to fight. Be encouraged and keeping going.

"I have fought the good fight, I have finished the race, I have kept the faith." (2 Timothy 4:7 NIV)

YOUR SACRED TIME, SPACE, AND CALLING

15-MINUTE FREEDOM EXERCISE

Avoiding the mess...sometimes it's easier to close the closet and not think about it. Then it starts to spill out of the door, and I have to do something about it. After the mess is cleaned up, I can sit and rest and feel a sense of accomplishment and peace. Then I look back at my house and see there is more cleanup to be done, maybe in another closet, or in the case of the other side of freedom, more freedom to be fighting for on behalf of myself and others.

One of my mentors is wonderful at reminding me to take time to stop, rest, and remember the freedom God has given to my family in the past and present and to celebrate His goodness. Yes, there is more to do, but don't push through without taking time to reflect with gratitude and praise. She challenges me to recognize God's character traits through what He has done for me; for example, how God saved, redeemed, defended, restored, strengthened, and loved me and was merciful and compassionate to me in a particular situation.

How about you? What do you think about taking time to remember what God has done? Or maybe you'd like to ask God to bring some freedom and restore some areas of your life. Think about setting aside 15 minutes to **Free(dom) Write**. In the future, maybe consider starting a separate journal, where you write the things you want to remember about how God redeemed your life, like stones of remembrance that you can go back to and reflect on. Write about God's character and faithfulness in those times. Write out your story. Write a prayer asking God to show you how He is fighting for you. Remember, when you journal, "just write," and don't feel like you have to edit or say things perfectly. I like to go back and reread my journal entries, and I find it encouraging and uplifting to remember what God has done. I hope you are inspired to do the same and that you are encouraged by these words—

"Oh, thank GOD—he's so good! His love never runs out. All of you set free by GOD, tell the world! Tell how he freed you from oppression, Then rounded you up from all over the place, from the four winds, from the seven seas." Psalm 107:1–3 (The Message)

SPECIAL TIME WITH GOD
Set aside 15 minutes. Read **PSALM 5** in the Old Testament. You may consider reading it a second time out loud. What verse sticks out or connects with you? Apply the SOAP Method.

S – Scripture – Write out the verse you chose. Write it in this space below or in your journal.

_____

_____

_____

O – Observation – What are one or two facts that you observe from the verse you chose?

_____

_____

_____

A – Application – How can you personally apply this verse to your life?

_____

_____

_____

P – Prayer – Write out a prayer to God related to your reading today. There is no right or wrong way to do this. Prayer is having a conversation with God. Think of this as a conversation starter between you and God.

_____

_____

_____

PRAYER AND ENCOURAGEMENT

Prayer changes things—**don't forget** the **power** of prayer!

A blind spot in my life has been fear. I didn't realize how much it affected me until I started writing this book. Fears began to surface more and more. It seemed like fear of failure and fear of success were somehow having a fighting match in my kitchen. Lies I had been believing about myself and self-limiting beliefs began to surface. Feelings of not being good enough or worthy of writing this book paralyzed me. The fact is, I'm not really a fearful person. Okay, I must admit, I do have a fear of spiders and do freak out when I see them. My poor family deals with the drama. On the other hand, I love downhill skiing. It's a sport where I take care and caution but love skiing double black diamond runs.

Pray! When fear knocks at my door, I've learned the best strategy is to take time to sit, pray, and journal about it. I ask God to speak to me about the fear, to help me to identify any lies I am believing, and to replace them with His healing truth and encouragement. I mentioned praying God's Word in this chapter and how effective we are when we do this.

One Scripture passage I like to go to when fear is rising up inside of me is Psalm 91. First I quietly read the entire psalm and then again out loud; then I like to say the words in the passage back to God like I am having a conversation with Him.

An additional way to pray is as you read the scripture, replace your name, or the names of your loved ones, in the scripture. This is a prayer method I've learned from devotionals from Lysa TerKeurst and Rick Warren and friends who call it different names. I like referring to it as the personalized method. Here's an example using Psalm 91 verses 14 to 16. Insert your name (or the names of your loved ones or people you are praying for) where I've placed my name, and pray/read it out loud. You can apply this to the entire psalm or any other scripture passages that resonate with you and that you find meaningful. This is also something you can add any time at the end of your SOAP devotional time.

"Because Kim (or insert your name where I've put mine) loves me," says the LORD, "I will rescue Kim; I will protect Kim, for Kim acknowledges my name. Kim will call on me, and I will answer Kim; I will be with Kim in trouble, I will deliver Kim and honor Kim. With long life I will satisfy Kim and show Kim my salvation."

Know that God's purposes will be accomplished in you by the power of His Word. In Isaiah 55:11 (NLT), God says, "It is the same with my word. I send it out, and it always produces fruit. It will accomplish all I want it to, and it will prosper everywhere I send it."

12

WHO ARE YOU?

"Free of all her guilt and rid of all her shame and known by
her true name…"

SONG CALLED "EVER BE," BY BETHEL MUSIC

THERE'S SOMETHING ABOUT sailboats that I find hopeful, inviting, and calming. I grew up near the water, and my parents often took us out on a family fishing boat on the weekends. We had a lot of fun, and I have fond memories of these times together. I remember as a little girl dreaming how I'd love to go sailing "On the Bay" one day. Then when I moved to a major harbor city in my university years, I thought of it even more. So when I moved to an even larger city to establish my career, I found myself yet again near water and a lake filled with sailboats.

The following summer, I took the next step in making this little dream a reality and signed up for a twelve-week "How to Sail" course. In this group program, we had access to a fleet of small keelboats, which are boats with a permanent keel rather than a centerboard. On each boat, we had an instructor and two or three students. The goal at the end was to learn how to sail on your own without the help of the instructor—not a small task in such a short period of time!

Each night we had homework to prepare for a written test and then a practical test scheduled for the end of the course.

I remember feeling flustered in the beginning and admitting to my instructor, "I don't know where the direction of the wind is!" Thankfully, he showed me some tips on how I could figure this out.

When it came time for the practical evaluation, my instructor and I ventured out into the lake, and he gave me some instructions to follow, similar to a driving test.

As we started heading back into the marina, I wondered if I had trimmed the sails properly and about the timing of my jibe and tack (jibing and tacking take you away from or into the wind[1]), and then the unthinkable happened.

I started to scramble as I realized I had missed a step.

"The boat's not stopping!" I yelled.

And before I knew it, we crashed into the dock!

Yes, the dock, which just happened to be connected to a permanent houseboat.

Yes, someone on staff's place of residence!

My instructor looked startled but didn't say anything. It then came time to go to our classroom and receive our evaluations. Since I went last, I had been scheduled to meet with the instructors at the end as well.

Hmm, I thought to myself, *I wonder if they've failed anyone before or, worse, banned them from sailing on the lake?!* My sailing dream seemed to now be a fleeting thought.

Then my turn came, and the instructor began to say, "You are the only one—"

Yes, they're going to fail me! I reminded myself as I slid down the chair slightly.

"You are the only one we are giving a designation with a..."

Wow, there's actually a name for ramming a houseboat with their expensive sailboat equipment! had been my next thought as I slid a bit farther down the chair.

"Congratulations, Kim, you are the only one we are giving a designation with a 'Skipper' rating in this group of students. The rest of the students this semester, which is normally the case, are receiving a 'Crew' rating. You have shown exemplary leadership skills out there and throughout this course, and we'd like to recognize you for them."

With absolute shock on my face, I then asked, "What about the houseboat?"

"These things happen," he replied and then shook my hand and handed me my certificate of completion.

My birth name, Kimberly, means royalty, ruler, and leader. I've struggled with leading others my whole life. It's not something a former people pleaser now redeemed thinks about. Up until a year ago, I often discounted my leadership style and let self-limiting beliefs stand in the way of my calling to lead and communicate my story and message to others.

I'd like to take you back nearly five years ago, when a friend recommended a book called *Your Secret Name: Discover Who God Created You to Be*, by Kary Oberbrunner, who I've mentioned is now thankfully a mentor and coach of mine. The book beautifully weaves three freedom-fighting and truth-telling stories together—the author's, the biblical character Jacob, and the reader, who is invited to discover the same kind of victory.

Through these stories, I learned how there are names that are given to us and how they have an impact in our lives. Names are incredibly powerful. We have birth names, which we received when we are born, and we have given names, which we inherit from the world, and they can be positive or negative in nature. Whether we know it or not, our names shape us. They impact the direction and the decisions we make for our lives. We can look to them for our identity and can miss the significant calling and purpose God intended for us. Your Secret Name is the one that makes all the difference—granted to you by the One who created you, and who has the best plan for your life.[2]

When I started reading the book, I knew my given name right away. It had been assigned to me while I was in my mother's womb.

A MISTAKE.

Not planned.

Not wanted.

Not blessed.

In some ways, I adopted the name MISTAKE for myself. It became my identity and part of my story.

In the healing and the freedom that God had given me, I knew that this name was not true. I have been chosen by God. How could I be a mistake? The truth in Psalm 139 says that I am fearfully and wonderfully made by God, who ordained all my days before one came to be.[3] And yet it seemed like the truth was in my head and not in my heart.

After reading the book, I set aside some quiet time to reflect and pray.

Now face to face in the presence of a loving and personal Savior, this time no voices were competing to tell me otherwise. No accusations were negating the truth.

As I sit here under your love and protection, Lord, who am I? What is my identity? I renounce the name MISTAKE; I don't want it in my life anymore.

As the truth started sinking towards my heart, I went on to say—

"Lord, you want me."

"You planned for me."

"You chose me."

"You bless me."

"Lord, what name do you call me? What is the Secret Name you have for only me?"

"Who do you say that I am?"

I waited for a response. It came later that day as I emptied the dishwasher. It seems like there is a tile on our kitchen floor where I often hear from God. It may sound crazy, but it's happened enough for me to see a pattern.

I call it my slow place.

It's one of the stops in my busy world where God seems to get my attention, often when I'm least expecting it.

When I heard the whisper, I knew. *Kim, you are loved.*
"Oh thank you, Lord—you love me!" I responded.
And then I thought about it more.
No, God's saying I "am" LOVED!
LOVED is my true name! My Secret Name is LOVED.

This new revelation marked the start of the most beautiful journey in becoming who I am created to be. It's like I had been trying to figure out who I was all this time while seeking and searching, sometimes in the wrong places, like I had been trying to figure out where all the pieces of a puzzle went, not knowing what picture I was making. And then I felt like God just handed me the puzzle box—and a view of the big picture!

This journey has been amazingly more than I could have ever imagined, made up in my mind, or even dreamed of. It's not been without hiccups and struggles along the way, but I'm thankful to have a real sense of peace, contentment, security, acceptance, and significance in knowing WHO I am and WHOSE I am in the process.

As my freedom and healing journey continues to unfold, God knew the name "LOVED" would touch and heal my heart and be linked to meaning and purpose in my life. My new name is one that I need to choose to walk in each day. Since I've received it, I'm not only "LOVED" but "LIVING LOVED" and now have a greater capacity to love and receive love—through God and others.

Revelation 2:17 (NIV) says, "Whoever has ears, let them hear what the Spirit says to the churches. To the one who is victorious, I will give some of the hidden manna. I will also give that person a white stone with a **new name** written on it, **known only to the one who receives it.**"

I continue to connect with the Your Secret Name (YSN) process so much that I am now a certified speaker and coach on the "Your Secret Name Team." The YSN message helps people walk in their true name and calling by creating a space for—

- A true encounter with a loving God. Far too many Christians see God as distant and removed from their lives. YSN shows them that God is intimately aware of who they are and that He wants to have a deep, intimate relationship with them.

- Major impact. People see themselves as significant members of God's family with valuable roles to play in His Kingdom.
- Discovering your true identity. All people are created in the image of God. However, very few understand who God created them to be.
- Engaging in an unpretending, honest conversation with a God who sees you, cares for you, hears you, and understands what you are going through.
- Transformed lives. When people begin to see themselves as image bearers of God, they begin to live with renewed purpose and determination.
- Finding a voice for your pain and asking God to speak to you through your feelings and emotions while listening for the truth and encouragement He has to say to you.

There is great value in speaking biblical truth over yourself and your loved ones. That being said, there is something that happens when we ask God to speak His healing truth over us. When we take time to sit with our Heavenly Father, engage in a conversation, and listen and hear what He has to say to us in prayer and through His Word, we experience a whole new kind of FREEDOM.

Know that God's words are gentle, convicting, kind, helpful, and loving. He challenges you to change your thinking.

He does not condemn or accuse you.

That's not God.

Shame says you are a mistake.

Guilt says you made a mistake.

God wants you to know WHO you are and WHOSE you are so that He can speak purpose, identity, and blessing into your life. All this starts with a relationship with a saving God and an honest dialogue with Him.

Romans 8:1–2 (NLT) reminds us that "...there is no condemnation for those who belong to Christ Jesus. And because you belong to him, the power of the life-giving Spirit has freed you from the power of sin that leads to death."

Imposter syndrome is what happens when you wrestle with believing in yourself. It's something that, if we are honest, we have all felt at some stage in our lives. We are not alone in our trials. We all have struggles and are on our own journey of pain. We place our identity in different things, such as what people think of us; people pleasing and performance-based living can become a way to survive and cope with life. We tend to wear masks, where on the outside is our public life and on the inside is our private life. The brave ones are the people who are courageous enough to remove the mask and admit they need help to close the gaps in their life.[4]

People that experience the imposter syndrome represent approximately 70% of the populations, according to experts.[5] They feel like phonies, and their greatest fear is that they are going to be found out. People believe there is a discrepancy between how others see them and how they see themselves. You feel people see you one way, and yet on the inside, you know there is a whole different story—you feel like you need to pretend on the outside and keep up the pretense.

People with imposter syndrome are often successful. Think about it—if you are not successful on the outside, do you really need to pretend you are, because people already know you're not?

Quite a number of actors have struggled with the imposter syndrome. One confessed they are only one breath away from being found out. It's been reported that an actress who received a Best Actress award struggled with being an imposter. She was consumed with thoughts that the Academy would find out and come to take her Oscar away from her. She was already successful. Can you imagine what she could accomplish if she did not struggle with imposter syndrome?

With imposter-type thinking, the falsehood is that as long as you keep up the pretense, nobody will find out. The shame and trying to cover the shame are big obstacles that will consume your time and drain the life out of you. There is another way. I've shared about how we are the best version of ourselves when we are connected to our Creator, Core, and Community. How much do you think you could accomplish when you are connected this way and free from the self-limiting beliefs and lies you believe about yourself?

There was no shame prior to sin. In the Bible, Adam and Eve were the first people to experience shame—imagine a spotlight shining on them just after they sinned in the Garden. It can be the same for you and me. Maybe you don't like to be the center of attention. Maybe you do. Either way, when you are on a platform, you stand out, and everyone can see you. My coach says the spotlight doesn't ruin you; it reveals you. Maybe your limelight moment is coming. How will you respond when it does? Will you say, "I'm hiding behind the curtain," or "Put me on stage?"

How do we, as Kary says, "Show up filled up"?

How do we overcome these self-limiting beliefs?

I've been sharing in previous chapters about the benefits of looking beneath the surface, taking time for self-evaluation, being the best version of ourselves, closing the gaps, fighting for freedom, and having Truth Tellers in our lives. How we see people and how we respond to the world are different once we have dealt with our self-limiting beliefs and imposter syndrome struggles. If we don't get past these barriers, they will sabotage our success, and we will potentially miss what God intends for us.

Everybody has these self-limiting beliefs—which are really lies you believe about yourself. When you are connected to the lies, you are connected to the liar, the father of lies. The enemy's plan is to attack, steal, kill, and destroy you. Any time you feel like your "best" is being destroyed, these are the marks of the father of lies.

Don't let the enemy deceive you or lead you astray.

Stick with Jesus.

Thankfully, the best news is that God's plan for your life is bullet proof—a non-fragmented plan that gives life and life abundantly. Jesus says, "I am the gate; whoever enters through me will be saved. They will come in and go out, and find pasture. The thief comes only to steal and kill and destroy; I have come that they may have life, and have it to the full." (John 10:9–10 NIV)

Ignore the shame when you feel the imposter syndrome rising up in you, and reject the urge to put up the smoke and mirrors. When harassing thoughts show up just before you walk on the stage of life, acknowledge them. Name the imposter syndrome for what it is. There is something empowering about that. There is a way to say you are struggling with being an imposter without discrediting yourself, and 70% of your audience can identify with you. When you lead with true authenticity, you have a story to tell, and you gain credibility with people because you are the expert on your own "real" story.

Let's think about King David again. Remember he was brutally honest with God? Shame keeps us from being vulnerable and says we are not worthy of connection, yet David is honored and welcomed for being authentic.
We can be assured that when we meet with and trust God with our struggles, we are greeted with His mercy and compassion—not disgrace but grace from a loving God who desires to set us free from paralysis and defeat.

This is exactly how you can break free from the imposter syndrome by being sincere and truthful about how you are feeling with God and others.

Here are some practical steps you can take to do this—

REPENT—This means to turn from and to confess and admit sin. This is a major step. When you are wearing a mask, even in your writing, people know it. Lead with vulnerability, and be honest about your imposter syndrome. God's forgiveness of sinners is dependent on their repentance.

RENOUNCE—What is standing in the way between you and God? Close the gaps. Confess and renounce the sin, lies, and masks you are wearing in God's power. Do this not in your own strength. Render it inoperative. Declare that it is no longer going to dominate you. "If we confess our sins, he is faithful and just and will forgive us our sins and purify us from all unrighteousness" (1 John 1:9 NIV).

REPLACE—You need to replace where the sin and lies have resided with something. If you plan to go on a diet, you still need to eat something. You have to replace it with the right food. It's the same thing with the imposter syndrome. When you say you are no longer going to be struggling with lies, what is the truth you are going to replace it with?

See Appendix C, where you will find the ABCs of Your Position or Identity in Christ. This is something you can write out in your journal or refer to in this book again and again. Read through the ABCs, and mediate on the truth to counteract the imposter syndrome and the lies you are believing about yourself. This is WHO you are in Christ. This is your position in Christ.[6]

Your position is WHO you are.

Your condition is HOW you are.

A secure position creates a secure condition. Take some time to look up the Bible verses on the ABCs list. Write them out in your journal. This will help you understand who you are in Christ. The more you can connect with these truths, the more your condition will begin to match up with your position, and you can be free to be authentically WHO you are in all situations.

We've been reading the psalms in our "Special Time with God," most of which have been written by David. I hope you've been inspired by his direct and to-the-point approach and will consider engaging in your own authentic dialogue with God.

In the book of Matthew in the Bible, there's something called the Beatitudes that starts with "Blessed are…."[7] The first one is "Blessed are the poor in spirit, for theirs is the kingdom of heaven."[8] "Poor in spirit" means spiritually bankrupt. When you see yourself as bankrupt—like financially bankrupt—you have nothing, you are in the hole, and you can't save yourself. Blessed are those who are in the hole and who can't save themselves for theirs is the kingdom of heaven.

So basically, our condition is desperate and hopeless. But your position, if you are a follower of Jesus, is secure, rock solid, unshaking, and unwavering. When you have a clear understanding of WHO you are—your position in Christ—your condition will begin to match up and reflect that. I know because I've struggled with people pleasing, leading others, my identity, fear of success, fear of failure, finding my voice, believing lies, and most definitely the imposter syndrome.

Is imposter syndrome something you can relate to?

How could overcoming the struggles in your life potentially be your greatest contribution to the world?

Do you see how the enemy would want to distract you from defeating the imposter syndrome?

Imagine if you were free from the lies you knowingly or unknowingly believe about yourself—how could you help, impact, and change the world around you?

"Every name has a story, and every story has a wound."[9] Get in touch with your story. Until you stop hiding, you can't break free from the names and the lies that are keeping you trapped.

Maybe you are avoiding God.

Putting off the conversation.

Hoping it will go away.

But God's been saying to YOU—

How can I help you?

How can I heal you?

How can I encourage you?

How can I bless you?

This past fall I attended an Igniting Souls Conference in Columbus, Ohio, and had an amazing opportunity to attend a Your Secret Name session led by Kary and his business partner, David Branderhorst. They both authentically told their freedom fighting stories and invited us to dig deeper into our own stories to discover more about who we were created to be.

As I've led others and myself on this topic, I've found when we take time to ask God about our identity and WHO He says we are, He encourages us again and again.

It doesn't stop; it gets better.

I think that's why He desires us to pursue healing and freedom—so we can be whole again to receive His love and blessing intended for us.

There has been this unfolding love story since I received my Secret Name. One day, standing in the kitchen again—remember my slow place?—I sensed God saying,

"You are living LOVED," and another time, "You, LOVE ME."

Wow, after all the healing and freedom God has given me, He has faithfully honored my desire to have a deeper relationship with Him. The way I see it is that God has given me a new capacity to receive His love and to love Him in return. It just amazes me how God works when we are open to what He has for us.

And so back to the Igniting Souls Conference, where at the end of this session, we had a time of personal reflection. In that moment, I sensed God saying to me these encouraging words—

"No longer a mistake. You are LOVED. You've done so much work on this. Sit with me and celebrate. ENJOY your freedom. Be still. Be with me. Stay awhile. The Given Names don't stick anymore. I am your Shield. I am your Defender—fighting the names off. You are blessed. You are My Beloved."

God is inviting you to sit with Him. Take off the mask, and take some time to talk honestly with Him.

Find a Slow place.

In Christ—

It's a Safe place.

A Loved place.

A Valued place.

You are God's choice. He says you are not a mistake or here on this earth by accident. You are honored, accepted, loved, and significant in His eyes. You are destined for great things because He created you for this time and this place. He wants you to be confident in WHO you are and WHOSE you are because He LOVES you and wants to BLESS you. God says this about you—

"But you are a chosen people, a royal priesthood, a holy nation, God's special possession, that you may declare the praises of him who called you out of darkness into his wonderful light. Once you were not a people, but now you are the people of God; once you had not received mercy, but now you have received mercy." (1 Peter 2:9–10 NIV)

Your Sacred Time, Space, and Calling

15-Minute Freedom Exercise
Who are you? Who does God say you are? Do you know God's new name for you? Would you like to experience "THE NAME CHANGE"? Before you start, a warning—this process will be more than 15 minutes, but it's so worth it! Take your time. Freedom is found here.

Step One: Give Your Life to Christ.
Have you ever given your life to Jesus Christ? In other words, have you acknowledged that you are a sinner, asked God for forgiveness of that sin, and placed your faith in Jesus Christ's finished work on the cross in order to receive salvation and the new life that He offers?

- If your answer is YES, then continue to Step Two.
- If the answer is NO, then take this time to accept Christ into your heart. If necessary, find someone who is willing to pray with you and

talk you through any struggles or questions you may be having about this important decision.

STEP TWO: REPENT OF YOUR GIVEN NAMES.

The Bible says that any person who is in Christ is a new creation; the old things (names) have passed away, and new things have come.

- Identify the name(s) the enemy is using to hold you down. (Remember John 10:10?) Spend some time alone writing down the names that come to mind. It is important to identify these names so that you can pinpoint the weapons the enemy is using against you.
- Explain your Given Names. What is your earliest memory of each name? Think about the circumstance surrounding the time this name was spoken to you and what caused you to believe it to be true. Every name has a story, and every story has a wound. Write down the story surrounding your wound.
- Repent of your belief in these names. No matter the circumstances surrounding your Given Names, they are not the truth about who you are in Christ. God sees none of His children as failures, mistakes, dirty, or undesirable. You are loved by Him and co-heirs with Christ of the Kingdom of God. Take some time to pray through each Given Name, and repent of believing it. "You were taught, with regard to your former way of life, to put off your old self [name], which is being corrupted by its deceitful desires; to be made new in the attitude of your minds; and to put on the new self [name], created to be like God in true righteousness and holiness" (Ephesians 4:22–24 NIV).

Sample Prayer: God the Father in Heaven, I confess that I have chosen to believe that my Given Name(s) is/are_____. I repent, Father, and now turn from believing this lie.

STEP THREE: RENOUNCE YOUR GIVEN NAMES.

Renounce means to refuse to follow, obey, or organize any further. Do you refuse to recognize and follow the Given Names that have been given to you and anything from the enemy attached to them?

- Bring the power of Christ into your wounds. Ask Jesus to come into this situation where you first received this name and wound. Ask God to speak His truth into your wounds. Remember that God is not full of condemnation but rather love and grace. Pray that the blood of Christ would be poured over you, and accept His healing for you.

Sample Prayer: I renounce the lie that I my Given Name(s) is/are _____. I refuse to recognize it in my life any longer and reject the power that it had over me.

Don't stop here! I've created a space for you under "Prayer and Encouragement" to continue on with these steps. If you are finding it difficult to work though these steps, pray and ask God to help you. Ask a trusted friend to pray with or for you. I'm praying for you right now as I'm writing this to you. You're doing great—keep going!

SPECIAL TIME WITH GOD

Set aside 15 minutes. Read **PSALM 139** in the Old Testament. This psalm is often referred to as God's love letter to us. I hope you are deeply encouraged and that you discover how much God loves you. You may consider reading it a second time out loud. What verse sticks out or connects with you? Apply the SOAP Method.

S – Scripture – Write out the verse you chose. Write it in this space below or in your journal.

_____
_____
_____

O – Observation – What are one or two facts that you observe from the verse you chose?

_____

_____

_____

A – Application – How can you personally apply this verse to your life?

_____

_____

_____

P – Prayer – Write out a prayer to God related to your reading today. There is no right or wrong way to do this. Prayer is having a conversation with God. Think of this as a conversation starter between you and God.

_____

_____

_____

PRAYER AND ENCOURAGEMENT
Continue **discovering** and **walking** in your **NEW NAME**...
   (See Steps 1 to 3 under "15-Minute Freedom Exercise.")

STEP FOUR: DEMOLISH YOUR GIVEN NAMES.
"The weapons we fight with are not the weapons of the world. On the contrary, they have divine power to demolish strongholds. We demolish arguments and every pretension that sets itself up against the knowledge of God, and we take captive every thought to make it obedient to Christ. And we will be ready to punish every act of disobedience, once your obedience is complete." (2 Corinthians 10:4–6 NIV)

Sample Prayer: In the name of Jesus, I erase, break, and bind the power, schemes, and attacks of the enemy regarding this name. In the name of Jesus and by the power of the Holy Spirit, I declare that the Given Name(s) _____ has no right or place in my life. (Take time to pray through each name.)

STEP FIVE: ASK GOD FOR YOUR SECRET NAME.

The Bible says that if you believe in Christ, you are an overcomer. Jesus has a new name for you and wants to give that name to you. (Read Revelation 2:17.) Spend some time in prayer honestly engaging God and asking Him to reveal your true identity—your Secret Name.

> Sample Prayer: Jesus, I know that you have a new name for me. You don't see me for the old names that I've believed. I ask you to reveal to me what my Secret Name is—the name that you gave to me.

STEP SIX: DISCOVER GOD'S SECRET NAME.

When we discover our own Secret Name, something odd takes place; we actually end up discovering one of God's Secret Names. The Scriptures often demonstrate God's people naming His unique attributes after experiencing His unique attributes.

- Hagar, the mother of Ishmael, upon realizing that God understood her unique situation, gave God the name El Roi. "She gave this name to the LORD who spoke to her: 'You are the God who sees me,' for she said, 'I have now seen the One who sees me'" (Genesis 16:13).
- Abraham, the father of the nation of Israel, upon finding the ram that God provided, gave God the name Jehovah Jireh, the LORD will provide. (Genesis 22:14)
- Moses, the deliverer of Israel, upon experiencing victory over the Amalekites, gave God the name Jehovah Nissi, the LORD is my banner. (Exodus 17:15)
- David, the king of Israel, upon experiencing safety through the valley of the shadow of death, gave God the name Jehovah Raah, the LORD is my Shepherd. (Psalm 23:1)

> Sample Prayer: Father, you've healed me from my Given Name(s) of _____. I ask you to now reveal yourself to me in a unique way. Please reveal to me my Secret Name for you.

STEP SEVEN: WALK IN YOUR NEW NAME.

Ephesians 4:22–24 tells us we must no longer walk according to our old name but rather in light of our new name. While seeing ourselves through the eyes of God for the first time is a powerful experience, it is the first step in a new journey. Oftentimes as a result of receiving our Secret Name, God places a new calling on our lives. Over the next several days, spend time in prayer asking God about the calling on your life.

> Sample Prayer: Father God in Heaven, you have shown me who you created me to be and have allowed me to see a glimpse of myself through your eyes. I pray now that you will show me how I am to further your kingdom in light of my true identity.

Source: The Name Game (with Insights from Mark 5:1–15) based on *Your Secret Name* by Kary Oberbrunner, published by Zondervan. These seven steps have been adapted with permission.[10] If you feel like you need to go deeper on the topic of your identity and discovering who you were created to be, be sure to read his book, *Your Secret Name: Discovering Who God Created You to Be.*

Another book I've found helpful is by Dr. Neil Anderson, called *The Bondage Breaker.* It has a number of helpful prayers, and if you are not familiar with it, consider looking it up online. If the topic resonates with you, it's worthwhile reading and praying through the "Steps to Freedom in Christ." If you do decide to pray through the steps that Dr. Anderson outlines, be prepared for some resistance from the enemy, who doesn't want you to break free from anything. I strongly recommend you ask a trusted person to pray with and/or for you when you are reading the book and praying through the steps. I know a leader who prays through the "Steps to Freedom in Christ" on a yearly basis—kind of like a spiritual spring cleaning or cleanse of sorts.

13

WHY ARE YOU HERE?

"The place God calls you to is the place where your deep gladness
and the world's deep hunger meet."

FREDERICK BUECHNER

"CAN YOU HELP me?" I asked my friend. She graciously responded, "I'd love to!"

Scheduled to speak at a conference in a few weeks, I had a gap I needed to close before I went on stage. The question as to "What would I wear over the three days?" had been consuming my thoughts. And so I asked this dear friend, who has a great sense of style, if she would consider helping me pick out some outfits.

Knowing that I'm not a big fan of clothes shopping, she suggested I search online to get an idea of what I like. I tried looking up something like "slimming outfits for short, overweight women." I later told my friend about my findings, and she responded, "Aww, that's not who you are." My response to her was "But this is how I'm feeling and where I'm at right now."

FREEDOM FIGHTERS AND TRUTH TELLERS

I found one magazine article to be particularly helpful. Some of the slimming ideas for women were to—

- Try boot cut style jeans or pants,
- A longer cardigan or blazer that goes past your hips,
- Or a sweater or suit jacket that fits in close to your waist (but not a garment that comes just below your waist or the top of your hips),
- Tops where the length goes past your hips (even if wearing a waist-fitting blazer),
- And longer necklaces to elongate your torso.

As simple as these suggestions were, I could now see why I liked how some of my clothes fit and not others.

With a wardrobe framework in mind, I then went to the mall to search for some new pants. I remembered a store that had slim-fitting jeans advertised. As I approached the entrance, a woman greeted me at the door. "How can I help you today?"

I noticed what she was wearing and enthusiastically shared, "You are doing everything right!"

She looked at me and smiled.

I went on to say, "Your outfit has all the elements of a great outfit, according to an article I read."

She smiled again. "Oh, well, this is my signature style."

"Your signature style? Please, can you tell me more?"

She then talked about how she styles her outfits and gave me some tips for when shopping for pieces of clothing for my wardrobe.

The next day I met my friend feeling more equipped to close this gap on how I felt about my clothes. We went to a store she recommended, and she suggested I pick out some items I liked and meet her at the back. I arrived at the change room with one sweater, and she had a stack of garments for me to try on. My friend was amazingly helpful, and I left with some great outfits. Some pieces I wouldn't have thought to try on but loved. And yes, I'm excited to say I now have somewhat of a "signature style" of my own!

Inspired by how freeing this all felt, I went home, cleaned out my closet, and gave away two-thirds of my clothes. I kept a third of my wardrobe and now have a filter or a framework—which is really a way of determining what's in and what's out when it comes to my wardrobe.

Shopping is so much easier now because I know what to look for. I'm thankful to my friend who helped me. When I went to the conference, I organized my outfits in advance, including jewelry and accessories, and I can't tell you how free I felt. Having confidence in WHO I am, truth to combat the lies, help from a friend, and a framework to follow, I closed a gap off stage so I was free to be me on stage.

When you get scared before a presentation or an interview and negative thoughts are harassing you, go back and reread the ABCs of your position in Christ (Appendix C) introduced in the previous chapter. Speak them out loud. This will help you tear down the lies and replace them with God's truth. It will also lift any confusion and create a space for you to discern next steps and practical ways to overcome the resistance that comes your way. For example, in my case, I thought to ask a friend for help and to go shopping with me.

Keep reminding yourself WHO you are in Christ and WHO God says you are. You have to do this because there are people who need your help and who need to hear your message. When you are free to be yourself, they will connect with you.

Have you ever felt defeated, discouraged, or distracted? I have. Have you lost your way? I did for a decade before I came to the end of myself. Do you know your why? I didn't.

An oversized interruption in my thinking occurred at an out-of-town conference I attended two and a half years ago. In some ways, I thought I was on track and living my dream. What I've come to realize is that there were times I was not fully dreaming. What I've learned is that with healing comes clarity; I was where I needed to be, and it was time for more clarity in my life. And when you know your WHY and your purpose for

FREEDOM FIGHTERS AND TRUTH TELLERS

being on this earth, your "reason" behind your dream and passion will pull you forward.

Sitting in a corporate business setting in Columbus, Ohio, I looked around, thinking to myself, *This is a dream come true, but why am I feeling anxious inside about being here?* I had been away from the corporate environment for some time now, but this type of setting would have been a regular occurrence for me. Was it just nervous jitters?

Then it came to my turn to share my name and where I was in the OPUS process. "Hi, I'm Kim, and I actually have two overarching visions for my life, and I am here to decide which one to choose."

My coach, Kary, said, "Tell us more."

"Well, I have a safe OPUS and a scary OPUS," I went on to say.

"What OPUS do you think you will go with?" was his next question.

"The scary one," I replied.

At this time in my life, I had experienced tremendous healing and transformation and was truly thankful for the purpose and passion that God had for me on the other side of this newfound freedom. In a way, I thought I was on track and living my dream. Which I was and I wasn't.

Here's a checklist we then went through that I found helpful. Maybe you can read through it and circle what is true for you:[1]

1. I don't know my OPUS.
2. I haven't discovered my voice.
3. I don't know what I truly desire.
4. I am listening to fear in some area of my life.
5. I don't know if my life is making a difference.
6. I am singing someone else's song part of the time.
7. Lack of money or resources is getting in the way of my dreams.
8. I feel disconnected from my Creator, my Core, or my Community.
9. I feel incapable of achieving the desires pumping through my blood.
10. I don't know who I am, why I'm here, or where I should invest myself.

As I read through this list, some light bulbs started going off. How about with you? Do any of these statements resonate with you? Personally, I came to the conclusion I had a few more gaps to close than I thought as a number of these concepts applied to me, the most prominent one being "I am singing someone else's song part of the time." Wow, this had been so ingrained in me from my past people-pleasing tendencies that I didn't see how it had been holding me back from my calling and purpose in life.

I keep mentioning this thing called my OPUS, and you must be wondering what, in fact, I am talking about. Authoring your OPUS is part of a powerful coaching model called "The Deeper Path," developed by my mentor and coach, Kary Oberbrunner, and inspired by his coach and builder, Chet Scott of Built to Lead. Through this process, I've personally received a significant amount of clarity and have since been certified to coach and mentor others in this same process.[2]

The word OPUS is a Latin word meaning "masterpiece." The Deeper Path is a process that provides practical steps that let your hurts lead to your healing and your potential. This transformational OPUS framework equips you to—

- Discover your Over-Arching Vision and BIG DREAM for your life.
- Determine your BIG DREAM Ingredients: Someone (Tribe), Something (Cause), Somewhere (Space).
- Know your Purpose, answer the question as to WHY you are here on this earth, and discover your Melody Line (the song of your heart).
- Develop Unifying Strategies: three to five strategies to say "YES" to and learn to say "NO" to the rest.
- Establish your Scorecard for Significance: Baby Steps to Your BIG DREAM.
- Strengthen your CORE: Worldview, Identity, Principles, Passion, Purpose, and Process.
- Make your OPUS POP: Specific monthly action steps to make your dream a reality.

I have to warn you, this is hard work. It's actually painful at times. Although, it is pain with a purpose. You need to create space and make time in your schedule to do this work. You can't do what God is calling you do to without margin and investment in yourself.

Learn to say "NO" to the good things and hold out for the great things. Take time to think and dig deep.

Take time to ask questions, seek wisdom from God, and listen for answers. This is work, but if you stick with it, it will benefit you your entire life. Like my signature style story I mentioned earlier, your OPUS provides a framework to help you balance when to say YES and when to say NO so you can live out your God-given vision and purpose. Just as I needed help from a friend to pick out my clothing, you need help from a coach or mentor who will invest in you and help you uncover the clarity you need. My coach Kary says, "There's a danger in clarity. Once you know what you want, you're dissatisfied with anything else."

The payoff to all this hard work is that when you have the CLARITY you need, it leads to COMPETENCE, which leads to CONFIDENCE, which leads to INFLUENCE, which leads to IMPACT, which leads to INCOME. The more you invest in yourself and others, the greater the return.

Here is a part of my OPUS I'll share with you. I've shared my BIG DREAM in a previous chapter. This is my Someone, Something, and Somewhere—

My Tribe – Imagine a tribe of people who have each been given a dream, an overarching vision for their life, and they are determined to not give up until they are living it. Imagine a tribe of people who have clarity of their purpose and calling and are building into and investing in themselves, yielding competence, confidence, and influence. Imagine a tribe of people who are honoring their values, and as a result, their time, energy, and resources are aligned with the vision they have for their life.

Imagine a tribe of people who have made the decision to go from...

Being stuck, overwhelmed, and broken hearted to...

Becoming aware and discovering hope and healing to...

Breaking the Cycle of Hurt and chronic pain in their lives to...

Being set free and having their burdens lifted to...

Finding passion, purpose, focus, and a BIG DREAM (the song of their heart) on the other side.

Imagine a tribe of people who desire to live in the freedom that comes in knowing their identity and their unique calling, passion, and purpose. Imagine a tribe of people who confidently pursue their WHY (their purpose) by taking action resulting in an engaged life, genuine transformation, and an everlasting legacy.

My Cause – Is one of a Freedom Fighter and Truth Teller connecting people to a Love that is calling their name. My passion is helping others NOT MISS what was intended for them by creating awareness and seeing potential in others they may not see in themselves. My passion is uncovering greatness and connecting my tribe to a process in discovering their WHO, WHY, and WHAT'S NEXT? in a Bigger Story.

My Space – A space where you can intentionally step out of your daily life to take time for and invest in yourself. This space is creative, welcoming, and warm. This is a place where you can dream and ask questions (about your origin, destiny, and purpose) and experientially learn more about yourself. Are you ready for what you were created for? FREEDOM is found here.

These days, I am singing my song—the one given to me—more and more. I have a deep sense of gratitude for having not missed this calling on my life and have a renewed sense of purpose to come alongside and coach and mentor others on their journeys.

The Deeper Path is not just any coaching model. In my previous corporate career, my team was part of a world-class coaching program that had similarities yet had some missing pieces, in my personal opinion. Asking crucial questions about your life, identity, purpose, destiny, and beliefs are foundational in determining the direction for your life. WHO you are and WHY you are here on this earth are deeply connected to each other. Having the opportunity to incorporate my faith in this framework has been a game changer and has accelerated my growth and helped me impact the world around me. Remember, I've been down the self-help road. On the God-helps road, asking for and being open to God's leading and direction in my life is of utmost priority.

Ask God to lead you. "If any of you lacks wisdom, you should ask God, who gives generously to all without finding fault, and it will be given to you" (James 1:5 NIV).

Be open to God's direction in your life. "He guides the humble in what is right and teaches them his way" (Psalm 25:9 NIV).

I think God has planted a desire in each one of us to know our purpose and to make a significant contribution in this world. There is a reason why you are here. There is only one of you. There is no one else on the planet like you. I believe that God created you with a unique purpose. I believe that God created you to make a major contribution to this world. I believe that God gave you a message that is uniquely yours to give. I also believe we each have a choice. I believe as much as God puts this desire in us, we have a part to dig deep and do what we need to do.

Like this book. There are a lot of good things I could be doing right now. Good things for the world, others, and myself. I've had to dig deep and push through the resistance to get to my laptop, which I just spilled my chai tea latte on. I would like to insert a sad face here. I've been doing everything I can to protect my Thursday writing day, and now my backspace is not working. Not a good place to be if you are a writer.

I just called my sweet husband, who graciously listened, helped me brainstorm options to get my computer fixed, and said, "I'm sorry it happened, dear."

And so I can take a deep breath and remind myself that resistance is good because it means I am on the right track.

And just like God does, He surprised me right here in this coffee shop—a Sacred Appointment of sorts. As I looked across the room, I noticed the beautiful woman who, seven years ago, sat with me (and my tears!) in church the night I discovered there was freedom available I didn't have. I just love connecting the dots and seeing God's goodness and how it weaves throughout our lives. So excited to see her, I shared how I'm writing this book about how God so powerfully transformed my life. She is a natural cheerleader and blessed me with her words of affirmation as well as some helpful marketing advice. God knew I needed this boost of encouragement to keep going. I am so thankful for Him.

Part of the dream God has placed on my heart is to share Him and share the faith and hope I have in Him. To connect others to His love for them. To share my God story.

If I could say one thing to someone that I might not see again, I would say I don't want you to miss what God has for you.

If you don't think God is there for you…

Ask Him to show you in a way that you can't miss.

If you don't think He cares for you…

Ask Him to show you in a tangible way.

He will. It's a promise.

I've said how I cried out to God for help. You can do it too! He's waiting.

Don't keep God at arm's length anymore. Don't let partial truths keep you from knowing the full truth that will set you free.

Acknowledge if there is a problem that needs solving in your life.

Take ownership and responsibility for your actions, attitudes, and beliefs.

Recognize that your hurts lead to your potential.

Release your pain, and heal from your hurts so you can discover your passion, purpose, and calling.

Break free from what keeps you from the freedom and all that God intends for you.

One of my favorite blogs to read is by Rick Warren, called Daily Hope. He says, "Don't waste your pain. If you hide it and hold it back, it doesn't do any good. But if you're honest with God and yourself and with other people, God can use the thing you hate the most in your life, that you're most disappointed by, and that you wish had never happened. God says, 'You can't change what happened to you. But I can use it for your benefit and for my purposes. When you're willing to share your brokenness, I can use it to help other people.'"[3]

I think we know deep inside when we are not living our purpose and calling. We make excuses. We compromise. Sometimes we give up or we are content to merely encourage others in the pursuit of their dreams. We sit on the sidelines, but our hearts ache for meaning and significance as well. We grieve at the thought of missing out and wonder if it's too late for our dream to come true. With God, there is no scarcity of dreams, purpose, and important assignments. God's economy is counter-cultural. There's not just one pie with a limited number of pieces. When all the pieces of one pie are gone, God simply gives His people another pie.

How can your story help others?

What is the problem your message is going to solve?

What problem can you help others solve?

What is the pain you want to relieve or the itch you want scratch?

What comes easy to you?

Do you have a solution to a problem that will change the world?

Are you a Freedom Fighter and Truth Teller?

With freedom, you have a choice.

With truth, you need to tell it.

When you are aware, you have opportunities.

Your WHY is linked to filling a deep need in this world.

WHY are you here on this earth?

Here lies your passion, your purpose, and the song of your heart.

"For I know the plans I have for you," says the LORD. "They are plans for good and not for disaster, to give you a future and a hope. In those days when you pray, I will listen. If you look for me wholeheartedly, you will find me." (Jeremiah 29:11–13 NLT)

YOUR SACRED TIME, SPACE, AND CALLING

15-MINUTE FREEDOM EXERCISE

You need to know your value and how you will meet the needs of the world around you. Something I've learned from my coach and share with my clients is writing out a value proposition statement. This type of clarity can be helpful in communicating your message.

Here's my value statement:

"I am a Freedom Fighter and Truth Teller who helps the defeated, discouraged, and distracted walk in a newfound freedom so that they can become all they're created and called to be."

How about you? What is your value proposition statement? Fill in the blanks below.

I am a _____

who helps_____

do or understand_____

so that_____

Clarity attracts. Confusion repels. When potential clients or people you influence hear your clear value statement, they will be more likely to take the next step and be impacted by your message.

SPECIAL TIME WITH GOD

Set aside 15 minutes. Read **PSALM 33** in the Old Testament. You may consider reading it a second time out loud. What verse sticks out or connects with you? Apply the SOAP Method.

S – Scripture – Write out the verse you chose. Write it in this space below or in your journal.

_____

_____

_____

O – Observation – What are one or two facts that you observe from the verse you chose?

_____

_____

_____

A – Application – How can you personally apply this verse to your life?

_____

_____

_____

P – Prayer – Write out a prayer to God related to your reading today. There is no right or wrong way to do this. Prayer is having a conversation with God. Think of this as a conversation starter between you and God.

_____

_____

_____

PRAYER AND ENCOURAGEMENT

"Your **word is** a lamp for my feet, a **light on my path**." (Psalm 119:105 NIV)

Do you have any meaningful scripture that God has placed on your heart? I've shared previously that one way to pray scripture is to personalize it. For example, Psalm 1 has been particularly significant in praying for my family this year.

Pray! Here's how you can personalize and pray Psalm 1:1–3. Insert your name or the name of your loved ones in the bracket. Pray the words out loud. Look to personalize other scripture when you are reading your Bible and using the SOAP Method.

Blessed is (insert your name).
(Insert your name) does not walk in step with the wicked
or stand in the way that sinners take
or sit in the company of mockers,
but (insert your name's) delight is in the law of the Lord,
and (insert your name) meditates on his law day and night.
That (insert your name) is like a tree planted by streams of water,
which yields its fruit in season
and (insert your name) leaf does not wither—
whatever (insert your name) do[es] prospers.

Wow, is this not encouraging? I pray it inspires and is an absolute blessing to YOU.

14

WHAT'S NEXT FOR YOU?

"This is God's way: putting extraordinary tasks on the plates of ordinary people so that ordinary people can see what an extraordinary God can do through them."

PRISCILLA SHIRER, *DISCERNING THE VOICE OF GOD*

HAVE YOU EVER felt stuck, burdened, and overwhelmed? These words describe where I found myself a year ago. As a former people pleaser now redeemed, the all-too-familiar feelings were like flashing lights telling me to STOP and ASK—what am I carrying that I'm not meant to carry?

It didn't take long to put my finger on the answer. I had been in the midst of transitioning out of a position that, a year prior, I thought could be my dream job. Although I had given advance notice, the "nice girl" in me felt a responsibility to wait for the role to be filled, which could take months.

This was not quite what my overwhelmed emotions coming to the surface had in mind. This delay would prevent progress. The reality is, I had been saying yes to what I really wanted to say no to. The clarity I had from authoring my OPUS a year prior was shining light on the paralyzing pain of not having time to pursue my BIG DREAM.

I had a voice yet felt voiceless. I felt secure in my identity, but something appeared to be hanging on to my identity. Can you imagine a butterfly ready to fly? It's flapping its wings yet stuck and unable to break free from its cocoon.

The very questions that keep me grounded as a person—

God, what do you want to do in my life?

What are you telling me?

God, what can I learn from this situation?

What are you asking me to do?

The truth is, I felt confidence in the direction I sensed God leading me, yet I was not actually doing what He'd asked me to do. The diagnosis wasn't good. I had a serious case of delayed obedience. Better known as disobedience.

The breaking point came. It felt like a heavy weight or pressure pushing down on me. The pain of not wanting to give any more to this administrative position became unbearable. The weight of doing this job in my strength, not God's strength, was crippling.

I reached out to my community to pray with me and for me. I needed to take some time, sit with Jesus, process my emotions, and ask God to speak to me through what I was feeling. Was all this coming to the surface for a reason? What do I not want to miss or need to learn from this experience?

As I've mentioned, I personally find that writing or journaling helps me get unstuck. May I share with you my journal conversation with God?

Lord Jesus, thank you for this needed time with you. I'm here to have an honest conversation with you. Thank you for coming close to me. I just want to sit with you. I don't want to miss your closeness.

Please, I ask for wisdom only you can give me. Direction only you have for me. Please guide me in my next steps because as you know, I'm clearly not doing so well. I only want to hear from you and no other competing voices.

The name Administrator comes to mind. It's a name that's been given to me. It's not a bad name. I remember a couple of instances when someone referred to me as the Administrator and I just cringed inside at the thought. I'm not sure why.

Like the story of Jacob in the Bible, I feel your closeness, and yet I'm wondering if some of the heaviness and pressure I am feeling is actually a wrestle between you and me. Like Jacob, I feel like you are asking, "What do I want?"

Lord, I know what I want. I want to give this name Administrator to you. I don't want it anymore. I confess and give the name to you. Please show me what I need to do to be freed from it.

The name has been something I've hidden behind for many years. Part of me singing someone else's song and implementing someone else's vision. An administrator role is not what you are calling me to do. Thank you that you have given me administrative talents. Thank you that you have grown my character as I have administered. Lord, I just don't want the role anymore. Help me to set boundaries so that I don't fall back into it in other areas of my life as well.

Lord, I am saying sorry for the times I have been controlling. I'm sorry and ask you to forgive me for self-sufficiency. Thank you for putting the brakes on in my life. I've been so scared and fearful of failure. Stuck and really hiding behind all of this. Trying to hold myself up so to speak so I could do what I was good at as opposed to putting myself out there and walking in the calling you have given me.

I can see how working in my own strength is kind of like a hamster on a wheel. I am sorry for all of this. Thank you for allowing me to learn and grow despite me getting in the way. What did I miss all these years? What did I miss by not stepping out into my calling and hiding behind administrating?

"LOVED" is the name you have given me and affirmed many times over the last four years. How does giving up the name administrator fit in? Please give me clarity.

I sat, waited, and listened. Here's what I sensed God saying to me in response:

Yes, Kim, you are LOVED as you walk in your new role. No longer administrator—now AUTHOR and LEADER and someone who helps others find and share their voice. This is how you will connect others to me. This is how you will continue to learn and grow and a means by which I will continue to heal you.

See how your friend this week was encouraged by you? This was me working through you. With ease. No burden. Not something you can take the credit for really. See what I can do through you? More than you can ever imagine—immeasurably more.

Here the Bible tells us about the benefit of God working through us—

"Now to him who is able to do immeasurably more than all we ask or imagine, according to his power that is at work within us," (Ephesians 3:20 NIV)

It's been said God doesn't call the equipped; He equips the called. Something I share with my coaching clients is that it's not as much the goal that's significant but who you are becoming as you are accomplishing the goal.

I'm all for change and transformation. I don't know about you, but when I feel overwhelmed, my first response is not "What can I learn from this?" I just want to ignore and push down the negative feelings rising to the surface. Interestingly, what I've noticed with this strategy is that in my effort to suppress or numb my negative feelings, something also happens to my joy and passion for what I love. It's like they get pushed down too. I've concluded that I can't push down the negative feelings and not equally suppress or impact the positive ones.

Something I've been encouraged to practice during this last year is asking myself these questions—

What energizes you?

What drains you?

What fills you up?

The answers have provided me with more and more clarity. I think they can tell us more about our purpose and sacred calling in life than we realize. For example, administrating is something I have a talent for, and there is always a need for it. It's easy for me to take on a project and do a great job, but before I know it, the switch flips, and it starts to drain me. Then add conflict to something I'm administrating and "I'm done!" It paralyzes me. But as energy zapping as it all is, it can be easier for me to do something where I don't need to stretch myself, where I receive encouragement and can easily promote someone else's vision. It's hard to sell my own vision. It's not easy putting myself out there. It's not easy to do the work that needs to be done. It's easy to hide from it and endure the energy-draining pain.

In my overwhelmed and exhausted state a year ago, I could have missed what God had for me. Thankfully, He captured my attention. Thankfully, the clarity from authoring my OPUS has given me a life-long tool to clarify what matches my overarching vision for my life and what does not.

Today I am more focused on what God is asking me to do. Could I share with you about His faithfulness and how He is orchestrating immeasurably more than I could have ever imagined in my life?

- As I've shared, a friend told me about a book called *Your Secret Name*. This book helped me significantly to understand and walk in a new kind of identity and freedom. At the time, I saw the author was having a conference in Ohio (a plane ride and a country away) that I wanted to attend, but the timing was not great with two small children at home. In November of this past year, I went to my fourth conference in Ohio. Kary, someone I didn't know when I read his book, has been my coach and mentor for close to three years now. This past visit I had the opportunity to speak on the conference stage and share about this book you are reading now (a dream I didn't know I had back then). And if you can imagine, the person whose book helped me experience more freedom in my life is the person who graciously has written my Foreword to this book about fighting for more freedom. I could not have imagined it would turn out this way. Immeasurably more!

- Three and a half years ago, I wrote in my journal, "lead a Bible study using technology." I had no idea what this meant. I didn't know what content I'd use or how to use technology to make this happen. This past year, I started a "Connecting to a Love Calling Your Name 21-Day Program™" and mentored and coached groups of people from the U.S. and Canada through an online program with resources and content I created. I could not have imagined it would turn out this way. Immeasurably more!

- Two and a half years ago, I took some time and gave myself permission to dream. I decided to suspend the "you can't do this" critic and courageously wrote out the BIG DREAM that had been placed on my heart. At this time in my life, God had already brought much healing to my life. Was this it? Was there more? More freedom? More healing? More purpose? There were aspects that I wrote in my dream that I had no idea how to do (like write this book) and miracles I did not think would ever be possible. Today, a lot of what I dreamed about is happening. I've seen what God can do, and I'm thankful and in awe of Him. To get to this place, I've had to be intentional about staying true to my OPUS and seeking clarity on my "WHAT'S NEXT?" on an ongoing basis. I've had to create margin in my life and say "No" or "Goodbye" to the good things and hold out for the great things God has for me. I could not have imagined it would turn out this way. Immeasurably more!

It's in our struggles and the desert times in our lives where God is preparing us for something greater. More clarity. More rest. More freedom. More healing. More peace. More purpose. More joy.

We can still feel tired and burdened in some way, whether we are in a high place on a mountaintop or in a dark valley in our lives. If you are finding yourself overwhelmed or stuck, Jesus says to you—

"Come to me, all you who are weary and burdened, and I will give you rest. Take my yoke upon you and learn from me, for I am gentle and humble in heart, and you will find rest for your souls. For my yoke is easy and my burden is light." (Matthew 11:28–30 NIV)

God is so close to you. He wants to have an honest conversation with you. He wants to sit and spend time with you. He wants to speak life and encouragement over you. Let Him exchange your burdens for His ease and rest, your plans for His plans and purposes for you. He's a good God who wants to do more through you than you could ever imagine you could do on your own. Immeasurably more!

What is God telling you? What is He asking you to do?

Don't delay. You don't want to miss this.

YOUR SACRED TIME, SPACE, AND CALLING

15-MINUTE FREEDOM EXERCISE

What are you carrying that you are not meant to carry?

Jesus says come, lift off your heavy burdens and place them on His shoulders. You don't need to carry them on your own anymore. Be open and teachable; listen and learn from Him! It's here, in this surrendered place, that we witness a sacred exchange of our weariness for His rest and a lighter version of what we've been carrying around. It's not that our struggles and burdens are gone or disappear. It's that when we are open to God's leading and direction in our lives, He teaches us an easier and soulfully restful way.

When I'm carrying too much on my plate, I often find myself feeling incredibly overwhelmed. Sadly, it happens more often than I'd like to admit.

Is it just me? Does the feeling of being overwhelmed resonate with you? I find I'm getting better at picking up on the signs. Something that helps me get unstuck is taking time to journal about my feelings.

Would you consider taking some time to reflect and journal on this question: "What am I carrying that I'm not meant to carry?" Share with God how you are feeling. Are you feeling overwhelmed? Ask God for help and for the next steps to process the heaviness. Ask what encouragement and truth He would like to say to you through what you are experiencing. Use your own journal, or write in the space provided, to record what thoughts are coming to mind.

SPECIAL TIME WITH GOD

Set aside 15 minutes. I can't tell you how much I appreciated Psalm 91 in this season. I prayed it often back to God, and He encouraged and restored me through it. Read **Psalm 91** in the Old Testament. You may consider reading it a second time out loud. What verse sticks out or connects with you? Apply the SOAP Method.

S – Scripture – Write out the verse you chose. Write it in this space below or in your journal.

O – Observation – What are one or two facts that you observe from the verse you chose?

A – Application – How can you personally apply this verse to your life?

_____

_____

_____

P – Prayer – Write out a prayer to God related to your reading today. There is no right or wrong way to do this. Prayer is having a conversation with God. Think of this as a conversation starter between you and God.

_____

_____

_____

PRAYER AND ENCOURAGEMENT

At the foot of the cross…

Draw a picture of a cross on your journal page or turn to Appendix D, where you will find one.

What situations, burdens, obstacles, names, or roles (in my case, I mentioned the administrator role) would you like to give up and give to Jesus? Give each one to Him—write them at the foot of the cross, and ask Jesus to carry these burdens or heavy items for you.

Then the best part—ask God to give you His rest. Ask to be filled with His love, joy, and peace. (Read Galatians 5:22–23.) Ask God WHO He says you are. Ask what name, role, purpose, or plan He has for you in this time in your life. Ask Him to show you when reading your Bible who He is and who He says you are. Declare that you choose to walk in your God-given identity. Keep seeking this clarity. Give yourself permission to dream and hope again. Ask God to help you and provide everything that you need to make your BIG DREAM a reality. Know that God can do immeasurably more in your life than you can ever imagine.

Pray! Ask Jesus to help you walk in His path for you. Confess and turn from anything that is getting in the way of your relationship with God and the peace and purposes He has for you. Ask Him for clarity, wisdom, and direction regarding "What's Next" for you on your journey.

15

A LOVE CALLING YOUR NAME

"Just think, you're here not by chance, but by God's choosing. His hand formed you and made you the person you are. He compares you to no one else—you are one of a kind. You lack nothing that His Grace can't give you. He has allowed you to be here at this time in history to fulfill His special purpose for this generation."

ROY LESSIN

THIS WRECKED ME when I heard it. The statistic was shocking to me. It's something that affects nine out of ten people in your town or area. This is life-giving information. I'll give you a hint: It's something that tugs on my growing missionary's heart. You see, if you live in North America, nine out of ten people where you live have not heard a clear message of the gospel.[1] Many have heard about Jesus but don't know the full story. Maybe this is you. Maybe, like me, your heart grieves at the statistic and you'd like to do something about it.

So what is a clear message of the gospel? I grew up in a home where thankfully I heard the gospel shared, but I didn't fully understand it. There was confusion and not the clarity God intended. I really struggled with these partial truths in my life. Maybe this is why God has given me a heart to encourage others on their journey of faith and help them gain clarity on this vital subject.

In searching for answers myself, I've found the best place to go is the Word of God. What does the Bible say? I started by reading the Book of John. This is where I think a lot of light bulbs go on for people. Here is where you can discover who Jesus really is and why He came to this earth—His purpose, vision, mission, and plan for His followers to prepare for His return. God's rescue plan for me and you…this is the gospel. The book of John may be familiar to you, or it may not be at all. Either way, please consider reading it, and be prepared to meet and fall in love with Jesus for the first time or all over again.

God will encourage you exactly where you are in your faith. Christianity is not about religion, which some people say will tie you down or restrict your personal and intellectual growth. The Gospel of Jesus Christ is about a relationship with a loving Savior, who actually wants the opposite for you—He wants to give you eternal life, to set you free from what holds you back, and to see you thrive and grow in your purpose and calling. I believe it's when we learn for ourselves WHO God is that we learn more about WHO we are and WHY we are here.

As a way that I serve in my church and community, I'm a discipleship coach who comes alongside individuals and small groups for a season and helps people establish a firm foundation as they grow and mature in their walk with Christ. Our church and connections ministry is exceedingly intentional about providing next steps for people on their faith journey. In the Foundations course I facilitate, one of the topics we cover is stepping from a place of uncertainty to a place of confidence.[2] It's such a gift to journey with people and see them discover the life, clarity, and truth God has for them.

In my *Daily Walk Bible* (NLT version by Tyndale), there is a devotional in the side margins. It says in reference to John 20:30–31, "Becoming a Christian is not simply joining a church, signing a card, or walking an aisle, though these can certainly be valid expressions of your faith and desire to become a Christian. True faith comes as a result of believing on Jesus Christ, God's son, to solve your sin problem. It is trusting him to do something for you that you cannot do for yourself. Have you done that? If you have not, what better way to finish your reading of the Gospels than by opening your heart to the Savior of who those Gospels speak: Jesus Christ?"

Romans 10:8–13 (NIV) reads, "But what does it say? 'The word is near you; it is in your mouth and in your heart,' that is, the message concerning faith that we proclaim: If you declare with your mouth, 'Jesus is Lord,' and believe in your heart that God raised him from the dead, you will be saved. For it is with your heart that you believe and are justified, and it is with your mouth that you profess your faith and are saved. As Scripture says, 'Anyone who believes in him will never be put to shame.' For there is no difference between Jew and Gentile—the same Lord is Lord of all and richly blesses all who call on him, for, 'Everyone who calls on the name of the Lord will be saved.'"

With the people I disciple, we spend time looking at what a healthy growth environment looks like and how it is correlated to your success and maturity in your spiritual life.

We all want to grow and make a difference, right?

As a follower of Christ, this happens over time, and with the benefit of God's grace and truth in our lives as we—

Connect with God—Discovering the Truth in the Bible for yourself and through the power of prayer. This is why I love the SOAP Method and having "Special Time with God."

Connect with Each Other—Helping and serving others in a local church community and being open to others helping you in areas of your life where needed.

Connect to Others—Finding your voice and sharing your story with others. This is an essential part of spiritual growth and maturity. Telling your old and your new God-redeemed story is part of the healing process and a way to connect others to Jesus.

If you are a follower of Jesus and have any uncertainty about your salvation or your position in Christ, I believe God wants you to establish a firm foundation in Him so you can boldly live out your calling and purposes for your life. If you have any questions about what I've just shared, please talk with someone who knows Jesus. Ask them to pray with you. If you are someone who knows Jesus, and, like me, you would like to know how to share your faith and a clear message of the gospel, pray that God will bring mentors into your life—people who are on fire for God and can help you learn. Consider taking a Foundations-type course at a Bible-based church to equip you to disciple the people that God brings into your path. Be ready for the assignments God has for you.

God amazes me. I am really in awe of Him. One of the gifts He has given me is to see the big picture for my family and others. I get such a kick out of seeing God working in people's lives. It brings me great joy and fills my heart to connect the dots and point others to His handiwork. As human beings, we long for meaning and purpose. We want to be part of something bigger. We long for our story to fit into a greater story. I love how God's big story runs through each of our stories and our lives.

Know you are not here by accident or a mistake.

God planned in advance WHY you would be here on this earth.

God's plan for His children is to speak life, identity, purpose, and destiny into their lives.

Sadly, we have an enemy who desires to sabotage the blessing that God has for us. As I've shared in my story, Satan's assault started early in my life, while in my mother's womb. The enemy, through others, thoughts, and attitudes, imparted shame over my life, saying, "No, you were a mistake," and "You are not wanted or loved." God says that's not true—"You are fearfully and wonderfully made" and "I have a plan and purpose for your life."[3]

This early attack on my heart makes sense to me now—my growing passion for God and His Kingdom was a threat. Know that the enemy seeks to destroy, confuse, and divide families. God's plan for families is that they have clarity, unity, and a sense of purpose and that they are blessed. If the enemy can break up and pit a family against each other, then they are separated from the purposes of God. It's heartbreaking when I think about it. I think it breaks God's heart even more. All is not lost. It doesn't have to be this way. Because of Jesus and what He did on the cross, God wins. If we humble and submit ourselves to God, He will restore what has been lost and stolen.

Know that God's not mad at us. He's not waiting to scold us or make us feel bad for the choices we've made in our lives. My Father in heaven is a good dad. He wants the best for His children. He wants us to make peace with Him so that He can speak life-giving words over us. He wants us to turn away from sin and what keeps us from Him so He can speak identity and blessing into our lives. He wants to restore to individuals and families what's been stolen. Read this Bible passage from the Book of Isaiah and be encouraged—

"Then when you call, the LORD will answer. 'Yes, I am here,' he will quickly reply. 'Remove the heavy yoke of oppression. Stop pointing your finger and spreading vicious rumors! Feed the hungry, and help those in trouble. Then your light will shine out from the darkness, and the darkness around you will be as bright as noon. The LORD will guide you continually, giving you water when you are dry and restoring your strength. You will be like a well-watered garden, like an ever-flowing spring. Some of you will rebuild the deserted ruins of your cities. Then you will be known as a rebuilder of walls and a restorer of homes." (Isaiah 58:9–12 NLT)

When we get hurt, we want to avoid being hurt again. When we are reminded of the hurt, we look to numb our pain, run, or try to avoid the pain or the people who cause the pain. We look to put walls up around our hearts to protect ourselves. The problem with this strategy is that we are agreeing with the enemy's plan and not God's plan. When we numb our pain and put up walls, we are also potentially blocking the healing, relationship, blessing, joy, purpose, passion, and LOVE that God has for us. God in His nature is LOVE. He is LOVE. God can't *not* be LOVE.

With the passion and purpose God has placed on my heart, how could I live out my calling if I thought I was a mistake? God knew I would need to know that I am LOVED. He knew there would be important people in my life who would not have the capacity to love me and that I would not have the capacity to receive love or to love them back. Maybe our hearts were just too bruised, hurt, and broken. Maybe we remind each other of the pain. Maybe we step on each other's pain. We just don't know how to break the repeating cycle, and so we fight or flight to avoid the conflict.

When I began my journey back to God and cried out and surrendered my life to Him, my life began to change. I could see God's plan for me and my own family clearer and clearer. As God healed and continues to heal my heart, I can see how my new name—my Secret Name, LOVED—is linked to God's purpose for my life. Sadly, I did not fully understand this until the last five years.

My prayer for my children and their children and future generations is that they know and love Jesus, know their position and WHO they are in Christ, and learn God's plans and purposes early in their lives.

A dear friend of mine has a huge heart to bless others, and she prays a beautiful prayer that her ceiling would be my floor. I pray this prayer for our precious daughter and our sweet son. That my ceiling would be their floor. I pray this same prayer for you, my friend.

You may be asking, "Does God love me?"

Or saying, "But you don't know what I've done or what's been done to me."

Know that God says to you,

"I have loved you with an everlasting love." (Jeremiah 31:3 NIV)

Know that you can never be separated from God's love for you.[4]

This year God answered a prayer and a promise that I've been on my knees praying the last seven years. The years mixed with hope and discouragement and everything in between—would there ever be any change? I'm incredibly thankful to be on the other side of a breakthrough after years of waiting.

If I have learned anything from what I'm about to tell you, it's to keep praying for the miracle that God has put on your heart.

If you've given up praying, start praying again.

Last summer I found myself in this place.

Can you imagine a prayer warrior who did not want to pray anymore?

Like I did, go and dust off the promise that God gave you so long ago.

Read it back to Him.

Ask God to give you a promise to hold on to.

Ask Him to breathe hope back into your sails.

He is working behind the scenes on your behalf. It's so hard in the waiting. Keep going. Be encouraged. God is faithful and will honor your faithfulness. May it all be for God's honor and His glory. Read these words He says over you—

"But you are my witnesses, O Israel!" says the LORD. "You are my servant. You have been chosen to know me, believe in me, and understand that I alone am God. There is no other God—there never has been, and there never will be. I, yes I, am the LORD, and there is no other Savior. First I predicted your rescue, then I saved you and proclaimed it to the world. No foreign god has ever done this. You are witnesses that I am the only God," says the LORD. "From eternity to eternity I am God. No one can snatch anyone out of my hand. No one can undo what I have done." (Isaiah 43:10–13 NLT)

Breaking the Cycle of Hurt is worth pursuing. Fight for what matters. What I've discovered is that the space and place where the hurt resides has the potential to be replaced with identity, passion, purpose, and blessing.

Breaking free from the hurt inside has freed me to connect to a Love that is calling my name and share this message with others. God has honored and continues to honor my four-word prayer so many years ago—"Free me to love." God is helping me break free and learn to love and receive love from

Him and others. God is helping me live loved before my husband and children and to leave a lasting legacy of love—a redeemed legacy in honor of a loving and holy God.

Can one person change and make a difference if everything around them stays the same?

When we fully understand the depth of God's love for us, our actions are different, and we are different. Our difference makes a difference in the lives of the people around us.

Are you connected to a Love that is calling your name?

A Love that loves you no matter what.

A Love that loves you at your very worst.

A Love that loves you at your very best.

A Love that loves you in your darkest hour.

A Love that created you on purpose for a purpose.

A Love that wants to trade your mess in for a masterpiece.

A Love that wants to set you free to be all you were created to be.

You matter to God. He knows your name. You are precious in His sight.

God is saying to YOU—

"But now, O Jacob, listen to the LORD who created you. O Israel, the one who formed you says, 'Do not be afraid, for I have ransomed you. **I have called you by name; you are mine.** When you go through deep waters, I will be with you. When you go through rivers of difficulty, you will not drown. When you walk through the fire of oppression, you will not be burned up; the flames will not consume you. For I am the LORD, your God, the Holy One of Israel, your Savior. I gave Egypt as a ransom for your freedom; I gave Ethiopia and Seba in your place. Others were given in exchange for you. I traded their lives for yours because you are precious to me. **You are honored, and I love you.**'" (Isaiah 43:1–4 NLT)

Listen to the voice of God that says, "I love you."

Do you know you are deeply LOVED by God?

Your story is not your own—it's for others that need to hear about your freedom journey. You matter, and your life has meaning. Perhaps this is the moment for which you were created. God has put you here on this earth for a reason. For such a time as this, you've been called.[5]

WHO are you?

WHY are you here on this earth?

WHAT's NEXT for you?

Know you are part of a Bigger Story. The world needs you to keep going and to take the next steps in breaking free and changing the world around you. I'm cheering you on! I'm so proud of you. Thank you for this great privilege of journeying with you. I once had someone pray God's blessing for His people in Hebrew over me. It was absolutely beautiful. I pray this blessing over you, my friend. Just imagine it's in Hebrew!

"The LORD bless you and keep you; the LORD make his face shine on you and be gracious to you; the LORD turn his face toward you and give you peace." (Numbers 6:24–26 NIV)

YOUR SACRED TIME, SPACE, AND CALLING

15-MINUTE FREEDOM EXERCISE

If you are in a hard place in your life and you are not sure what to do, turn to Jesus. When I'm struggling, I've found the best strategy is to open my Bible and discover what encouragement and wisdom God has for me that day. On tough days, I also like to play worship music in our home or in my car. I can't tell you how much this lifts me up. And sometimes I just need to be in a quiet place to journal and listen to what God has to say to me.

Take some time to listen to what God is saying to you in this moment. Put on a worship song if you would like. One I'd suggest that you can search for online is "Oceans" by Hillsong United. Write down what comes to mind or is on your heart in the space provided or in your journal. It's okay if you don't hear anything to start. It takes time and practice to hear God's voice. What thoughts or encouragement do you sense God impressing on you? Go back to this encouragement when you are struggling. God speaks to us with truth and in love. If we are sensing something other than this, we can be assured it is not from Him. Ask God to help you tune out the discouragement and tune in to the life-giving words He has for you.

_____

_____

_____

_____

_____

_____

SPECIAL TIME WITH GOD

Set aside 15 minutes. Read **PSALM 107** in the Old Testament. You may consider reading it a second time out loud. What verse sticks out or connects with you? Apply the SOAP Method.

S – Scripture – Write out the verse you chose. Write it in this space below or in your journal.

_____

_____

O – Observation – What are one or two facts that you observe from the verse you chose?

_____

_____

A – Application – How can you personally apply this verse to your life?

_____

_____

_____

P – Prayer – Write out a prayer to God related to your reading today. There is no right or wrong way to do this. Prayer is having a conversation with God. Think of this as a conversation starter between you and God.

_____

_____

_____

PRAYER AND ENCOURAGEMENT

"**One thing** I ask of the LORD, this only do I seek: that I may dwell in the house of the LORD all the days of my life," (Psalm 27:4a NIV)

Our family is incredibly blessed to have the opportunity to attend a Christian retreat center in the summer. Today the leader at one of the sessions asked, "If you were to ask God today 'one thing,' what would it be?" Thankfully, God doesn't limit us to one thing. For me personally, my answer came to me right away. I'm praying for another miracle—something only God can do. How about you? What's your "one thing"? Take a couple of minutes to think about it and write it down here.

_____

_____

_____

Pray! Give your "one thing" to your Father in Heaven, and ask for His help, wisdom, and direction.

Before this last chapter ends, can I pray for you?

Lord Jesus, Thank you for the gift of journeying with this dear individual who is reading my book. Thank you for helping me share my freedom story with them. May they be richly blessed and encouraged to share their story with others. I pray that all that's been declared in heaven for them would take place here on earth. If they don't know you, Jesus, I pray that they would meet you. If they do know you, please build them up and strengthen them. I pray each person who reads this book knows that they are precious in your sight. That they are loved with an everlasting love. I pray for an abundance of faith, courage, hope, and perseverance to live out their purpose, BIG DREAM, and calling. Encourage them. Bless them. Protect them. Bring people into their life that will invest and pour into them. Restore their identity, purpose, relationships, and anything that been lost or stolen. Fill them with love, joy, peace, patience, gentleness, kindness, faithfulness, goodness, and self-control. Please do whatever it takes for their freedom and for your glory. In your Mighty and Precious Name, Jesus, Amen.

APPENDIX A

The SOAP Bible Study Method

What to Expect...

At the end of each chapter, we will be learning and applying the 4-Step SOAP Bible Study Method. SOAP is easy to remember and practical, and it provides a framework to connect in a meaningful way with God in His Word.

Think of this journey as a special time between you and God, just for you. You may find as you go along that you are thinking about people you care about and how this would benefit them in their lives. This is good. What you want to keep in mind, however, is how to apply God's Word and what you are learning to your life first. I encourage you to keep bringing yourself back to this and to make it a challenge for yourself.

Devotional time with God is so important. Pick a time when you are at your best—morning, afternoon, or evening. My favorite space and place to meet with God is with a cup of tea at the kitchen table.

All You Will Need...

All you will need is a Bible (physical or virtual), paper (preferably a notebook or journal), and a pen. The SOAP Bible Study Method is a journal method, and my hope is that it will encourage you to journal and even write more. I love how the creative process of writing helps us get unstuck when we are in need of change and inspiration.

If you find you are distracted or you do not have time to fit this into your schedule, pray and ask for God's help, and then look to establish a set time (plan for 15 minutes or longer if you prefer) each day. Or another option is that you can decide to set aside a larger period of time to read two or three psalms and apply the SOAP Method to each chapter. The key is to be intentional about spending this time with God. It may be a challenge to push through the resistance at first; however, the benefits of doing so will be long lasting. I'm praying for you.

SOAP EXPLAINED...

At the top of your journal page, write the date and choose your own title for your reading. Keep your writing to one journal page.

Date:

_____Title:_____

Step 1 – Write S for Scripture on your journal page.
> Read a chapter or a paragraph of Scripture. Select a verse that stands out or is meaningful to you. Aim to pick one verse and write it in your journal. Writing the full verse out is key.

Step 2 – Write O for Observation on your journal page.
> Write here what you observe from the verse. What are the facts?

Step 3 – Write A for Application on your journal page.
> What about this verse is resonating with you? How can you apply it to your life?

Step 4 – Write P for Prayer on your journal page.
> Write a prayer to God. Thank God, and ask Him for help where you need it. Your prayer can be long or short. There is no right or wrong way to do this. This is a conversation between you and God.

Appendix B

Your Psalm or Letter to God

_____

_____

_____

_____

_____

_____

_____

_____

_____

_____

_____

_____

_____

_____

_____

_____

_____

_____

_____

_____

_____

_____

_____

_____

_____

_____

_____

APPENDIX C

SOURCE: YOUR SECRET NAME

THE ABC's OF MY POSITION

I AM...

Accepted in the Beloved	- Ephesians 1:6
Bought with a Price	- 1 Corinthians 6:20
Crucified with Christ	- Galatians 2:20
Dwelt by the Holy Spirit	- 1 Corinthians 3:16
Enslaved to God	- Romans 6:22
Freed from slavery to sin	- Romans 6:18
God's Child	- Romans 8:14
Heir of God's Riches	- Galatians 4:6-7
In Him Complete	- Colossians 2:10
Jesus' chosen inheritance	- Ephesians 1:4
Kingly Priest	- 1 Peter 2:9
Light of the World	- Matthew 5:14
Mastered no longer by Sin	- Romans 6:14
New Creation	- 2 Corinthians 5:14
One spirit with the Lord	- 1 Corinthians 6:17
Perfect in Christ	- Hebrews 10:14
Quieted in the reality of who God is	- Psalm 46:10
Raised up with Him	- Ephesians 2:5-6
Seated in Heavenly places w/ Christ	- Ephesians 2:5-6
Transformed into the image of Christ	- 2 Corinthians 3:18
United to the Lord	- 1 Corinthians 6:17
Victorious through my Lord	- 1 Corinthians 15:57
Wonderfully made	- Psalm 139:14
Xpistos (greek for Christ) workmanship	- Ephesians 2:10
Yoked with righteousness	- 2 Corinthians 6:14
Zealous of good works	- Titus 2:14

APPENDIX D

At the Foot of the Cross

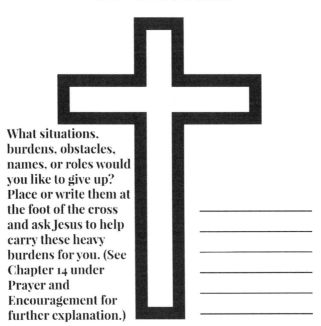

What situations, burdens, obstacles, names, or roles would you like to give up? Place or write them at the foot of the cross and ask Jesus to help carry these heavy burdens for you. (See Chapter 14 under Prayer and Encouragement for further explanation.)

ACKNOWLEDGMENTS

MY HEART IS full of joy. Lord Jesus, my love and praise for YOU will forever be part of my story. Thank you for healing my broken heart and setting me free to love and be me.

Doug, you are a genuine man of God, who is supportive, loving, and confident in who you are. You are one of the most supportive and generous people I know. I'm blessed beyond words to be your wife, I love you, and I am incredibly thankful to have you in my life.

Grace and John, you are SO beautiful and precious to me—both truly a blessing and a gift from God. Being your mom is the best assignment I've ever had and the greatest privilege. Through you, I've learned what it means to love unconditionally. I love you both to infinity and beyond and to heaven and back again. You are the means by which God got my attention and made me aware of my deepest wounds. It is for you that I made the decision to Break the Cycle of Hurt. I pray that you both fully understand how deep and wide God's love is for YOU. I'm so proud of you both. I believe in you. I'm your biggest fan!

Mom and Dad, thank you for choosing life for me. It must not have been an easy time for you in the early years of my life. Thank you for the times you supported me when my heart was broken. Mom, thank you for your devotion over the years in sharing your faith in God with me. I love you both.

To the people who supported and helped me to write and publish this book, a heartfelt thank you:

Kary and David, thank you for coaching and mentoring me these past three years and for helping me uncover this dream to write a book. How grateful I am for your generous support, belief, and investment in me. You both model what it means to fully live out your God-given calling and purpose. You inspire me to be a Freedom Fighter and Truth Teller—and to follow my Creator with all my heart. Thank you to the Igniting Souls Tribe and for the opportunity to be a part of the Author Academy Elite Program.

Merry, thank you for being a catalyst in my decision to Break the Cycle of Hurt and for being open to God working through you and positively impacting so many lives.

Rose Lynn, thank you from the bottom of my heart for our many discussions about this book and how you've challenged me to stretch and grow. Thank you for helping me connect with God in such a meaningful way and for your ongoing mentorship and investment in me. I appreciate you and how you generously share your gifts of wisdom, prayer, and encouragement.

Thank you to my dear friends—Dawn & Brett, Leanne & James, Amy & James, Pat & Doug, Elke & David, Dayna & Travis, Patti, Tracy, Beth, Tania, Lisa, Nathalie, and Fran—for your hearts and willingness to pray this past year as I wrote this book. Thank you to those of you who read an advanced copy and provided such helpful and encouraging feedback. I'm thankful for and adore each of you. Thank you for your constant words of encouragement, friendship, and support. You're amazing!

Patty, thank you for being an ongoing source of encouragement and for your generous heart to care for and pray for my family. Thank you for your support and for being the first person to read my book. You've helped and blessed me more than you know.

Kaelyn, Pat, Debi, and Carla—my beautiful friends. I love how God brought us together. Your hearts are so open and rich for God. Thank you for our life-giving conference calls, your cheerleading, and your prayers. You modeled to me how to share my message with the world. Thank you for sharing your hearts and stories with me. You inspired me to keep going. You helped me find my writer's voice. You blessed me with your words.

Michelle, thank you for going above and beyond in using your gifts and talents to help me make this book dream a reality! You are such a blessing, and I'm so incredibly grateful for you!

Carol and Daphne, thank you for sharing your encouragement, expertise, and editing gifts with me. You've blessed me beyond words.

Thank you to all the pastors, elders, staff, ministries, our small group, and our C4 Church family who have served, invested in, and loved my family and me in so many ways.

Lorie and Josea, you inspire me with your incredible hearts to connect others to God and community. Thank you for investing in and equipping me to lead, share my faith, and coach and disciple the people God brings in my path. I am so grateful for your support!

Thank you to Elim Lodge Christian Resort! For the past five years, you've been a soft place for my family to land. Elim is such a life-giving place, where we find genuine rest for our souls, have fun, get recharged, grow, and feel equipped to go and live out our purpose and calling in the world.

Thank you, Patti & Graham, Ingrid, and Leanne for your friendship and your encouragement at Elim and for helping me decide on the cover for my book. Thank you Bev & Earl, Ron & Susie, Colleen, and Marnie for your faithful hearts to pray for all that God intends for this book.

A special thank you to my Iron Group. Thank you for inspiring me to become a better writer! What an unexpected gift to be a part of this group.

Thank you to the beautiful women from my Connecting to a Love Calling Your Name 21 Day Programs ™ and Freedom Coach Programs ™. Your hearts to grow deeper in your calling and relationship with God inspired me to keep writing and to see this book dream become a reality. What a gift to journey alongside each of you and see how God is moving in your lives. Your enthusiasm to follow Jesus is truly contagious.

And to my readers—what a gift you are! Your hearts to fight for freedom and become all that you're created and called to be is such an inspiration to me. Keep going and pursuing everything that God intends for you!

NOTES

Chapter 1

[1] For further information on the "Elephant Thinking" concept, see http://www.freepromotips.com/article/do-you-suffer-elephant-thinking.

[2] The Shawshank Redemption. Dir. Frank Darabont. By Frank Darabont. Perf. Tim Robbins, Morgan Freeman, Bob Gunton, and James Whitmore. Columbia Pictures, 1994.

[3] John 10:10

[4] Read more about the Ten Commandments in Exodus 20:1–21.

[5] For encouragement and to read two of the hundreds of examples where God says, "Do not fear," "Don't be afraid," or "Fear Not," in the Bible, read Isaiah 41:10 and Isaiah 43:1–5. Take time in your devotions to search in the Bible for other examples.

Chapter 2

[1] For further info on Imprecatory Psalms, see http://www.gotquestions.org/imprecatory-prayer.html.

[2] Chet Scott spoke at Igniting Souls Conference, November 2014. More info at www.builttolead.com.

[3] The 21 Irrefutable Laws of Leadership: Follow Them and People Will Follow You Hardcover – September 18, 1998

Chapter 3

[1] See Wall Street Journal article at this link: http://guides.wsj.com/management/recruiting-hiring-and-firing/should-i-rank-my-employees/

[2] C.S. Lewis, Mere Christianity pg. 28-29 Lewis, C. S. (2014-01-02). Mere Christianity (Kindle Locations 19-21). Green Light. Kindle Edition

Chapter 5

[1] What Happens When Women Say Yes to God: Experiencing Life in Extraordinary Ways Paperback – Mar 1 2007 by Lysa Terkeurst. Find more info here: http://lysaterkeurst.com/wp-content/uploads/pdf/How_to_Hear_Gods_Voice.pdf

[2] LEWIS, C.S. (2014-06-28). C. S. LEWIS CHRISTIAN COLLECTION: Nine books including: Mere Christianity; Screwtape Letters; Miracles; The Great Divorce; Pilgrim's Recess; The Problem … (Timeless Wisdom Collection Book 1016) (Kindle Locations 2234-2235). Business and Leadership Publishing. Kindle Edition.

Chapter 6

[1] From a talk by Dr. Merry Lin, Breaking the Cycle of Hurt—Healthy Family Relationships. See http://www.drmerrylin.com

Chapter 7

[1] Quote posted by Kary Oberbrunner on his Igniting Souls Tribe Facebook Page, November 2014.

[2] Quote posted by Christine Caine on her Facebook page on November 29, 2014 https://www.facebook.com/theChristineCaine/photos/a.10150570623045089.648440.143678730088/10154895405735089/

Chapter 8

[1] This CPR course I took is referred to as CPRT (Child Parent Relationship Therapy) and is taught/facilitated by trained counselors and therapists. It was offered at a local Christian Counseling Center.

² See Psalm 139:4

³ Dr. Ron Gannet wrote *The Jesus Passages: Exploring the Words of Jesus Through Journaling* Paperback – Nov 20 2012. For more info see www. readthebiblewithus.com/about/

⁴ Questions from Kary Oberbrunner's book, *The Deeper Path: Five Steps That Let Your Hurts Lead to Your Healing*, Baker Books, page 157-178, see www.deeperpathbook.com

⁵ For more information on Brett Ullman and for a complete listing of his talks, please see www.brettullman.com

Chapter 9

¹ Definition of the word "mission" searched on Google at https://www. google.ca/?gfe_rd=cr&ei=RhnpVe_0JKOC8QevoJ3oBw&gws_rd=ssl - q=definition+of+mission

² Quote by Michael Hyatt—see http://www.michaelhyatt.com.

³ I heard Dr. George Murray speak at Elim Lodge Christian Resort Center. He is the Chancellor of Columbia International University. See for more info http://www.ciu.edu/discover-ciu/who-we-are/faculty-staff/ george-w-murray.

Chapter 10

¹ John C. Maxwell Quote from http://www.goodreads.com/quotes/57938- everything-begins-with-a-decision-then-we-have-to-manage. See www. johnmaxwell.com for more info.

² See John 19:30

[3] For encouragement, read Matthew 19:26.

Chapter 11

[1] Beth Moore, Breaking Free: Discovering the Victory of Total Surrender, B&H Publishing Group, 2000, page 71.

[2] The Daily Walk Bible, New Living Translation Second Edition, Tyndale Publishing House, Inc. Page 1513.

[3] Quote from Stormie Omartian's Facebook Page, where she posted on August 21, 2014.

[4] Quote by Stormie Omartian http://www.goodreads.com/quotes/635440-the-battle-for-our-lives-and-the-lives-and-souls.

Chapter 12

[1] http://www.dummies.com/how-to/content/how-to-jibe-and-tack-when-sailing.html

[2] For more information, read Your Secret Name: Discovering Who God Created You To Be by Kary Oberbrunner, Zondervan Trade Books, 2010.

[3] Psalm 139 verses 14 and 16.

[4] Summarized from Igniting Souls team call led by Coach Kary Oberbrunner on the topic of Imposter Syndrome.

[5] See Toronto Star Article http://www.thestar.com/life/2007/07/14/behind_the_mask.html

[6] Oberbrunner, Kary (2010-09-07). Your Secret Name: Discovering Who God Created You to Be (Kindle Locations 2235-2237). Zondervan. Kindle Edition, from Appendix 3.

⁷ Matthew 5:1–12

⁸ Matthew 5:3 NIV

⁹ Quote by Kary Oberbrunner, Igniting Souls Team Call, August 5, 2014.

¹⁰ The Name Game, See http://www.yoursecretname.com/wp-content/up-loads/2011/02/The-Name-Change-Personal.pdf for a copy of this free resource.

Chapter 13
¹ Checklist from Deeper Path Conference manual, Columbus, Ohio, led by Kary Oberbrunner, March 2013.

² For more information, see Kary Oberbrunner at www.karyoberbrunner.com or www.deeperpathbook.com and Chet Scott, Built to Lead, www.builttolead.com.

³ One of my favorite blogs is Rick Warren's Daily Hope. This quote is from September 12, 2014.

Chapter 15
¹ Based on a talk by Dr. George Murray, Elim Lodge Christian Resort, August 2013.

² Based on resources from Campus Crusade, Life Concepts www.cru.org.

³ Read Psalm 139 and Jeremiah 11:13–14.

⁴ For encouragement, read Romans 8 and in particular verse 38.

⁵ "For such a time as this"—see Esther 4:14.

ABOUT THE AUTHOR

Kim Gowdy is a Freedom Fighter and Truth Teller who helps the defeated, discouraged, and distracted walk in a newfound freedom to become all they're created and called to be. Kim's melody line—the song of her heart—is Connecting People to a Love That Is Calling Their Name.

In Kim's own life, she reached a point where she felt tired, burdened, and overwhelmed. In seeking out change, she was given perspective on how cycles of pain, hurt, and the lies she believed about herself played out in her life. Kim is incredibly thankful for her journey to wholeness and the opportunity to share her freedom story.

She is a Founding Partner and Certified Deeper Path, Your Secret Name, and Dream Job Coach. Kim is married and blessed with two precious children. Connect with her at www.KimGowdy.com.

Let's keep
the conversation going...

We have a round table in our kitchen which has four comfy chairs around it. We call it the cottage table because it came from my parents-in-law's cottage. When people come to our house, they all gravitate around the table and we often end up adding more chairs. My hope for this book has been that it would be like having you over to my house for a cup of tea around our table and having a heart to heart chat about our freedom fighting stories.

I may not know you by name, but I'd love to. It would mean so much to keep in touch and to hear how God is moving in your life.

If you visit my website at www.KimGowdy.com, ♥ we can stay connected.

Thank you and Blessings to YOU.

Kim

P.S. If you were inspired by **Freedom Fighters and Truth Tellers: Breaking Free From the Hurts Inside So You Can Change the World Around You** and desire to start, or deepen your own personal relationship with Jesus Christ, I encourage you to find a mentor who knows Jesus, or a Bible believing local church in your area. Please also refer to my website for additional resources.

Let's Stay Connected at
KimGowdy.com

If you liked this book...

♥ Tell your friends by going to
www.kimgowdy.com/freedom and clicking "**LIKE**"

♥ Go to facebook.com and find my **Kim Gowdy Author Page**, click "LIKE" and post a comment regarding what you enjoyed about the book

♥ Tweet "I recommend reading **#freedomfightersandtruthtellers** by @kim_gowdy "

♥ Hashtag **#freedomfightersandtruthtellers**

♥ Subscribe to free resources at **www.kimgowdy.com**

FREEDOM FIGHTERS AND TRUTH TELLERS

Connecting people to a Love that is calling their name

Do you long for a deeper relationship with God?

Do you have an important assignment or
a sacred calling on your life?

Do you long for significance, purpose,
and to make a difference in the world?

Do you want to be a part of a Bigger Story?

Imagine author Kim Gowdy leading
you through a series of
transformational processes.

Imagine finding clarity and
overcoming defeat by discovering
WHO you were created to be.

Imagine finding clarity and overcoming discouragement by
discovering **WHY** you are here on this earth.

Imagine finding clarity and overcoming distraction by
discovering **WHAT's NEXT** in making your **BIG DREAM** a reality.

Go to **KimGowdy.com** for great resources and
details regarding upcoming
Freedom Coach Programs™

Made in the USA
Charleston, SC
18 October 2016